Literary Angels

Literary Angels

Edited by

HARRIET SCOTT CHESSMAN

FAWCETT COLUMBINE
New York

A Fawcett Columbine Book
Published by Ballantine Books
Copyright © 1994 by Harriet Scott Chessman

All rights reserved
under International and Pan-American
Copyright Conventions.
Published in the United States by Ballantine Books,
a division of Random House, Inc., New York,
and simultaneously in Canada by Random House of Canada Limited, Toronto.

Owing to limitations of space, permissions acknowledgments appear on page 272

Library of Congress Catalog Card Number: 94-94355

ISBN: 0-449-90774-0

Cover design by David Stevenson
Cover illustration by Michael Deas
Book design by Ruth Kolbert

Manufactured in the United States of America

First Edition: November 1994

10 9 8 7 6 5 4 3 2 1

FOR

Marissa, Micah, and Gabriel

CONTENTS

ACKNOWLEDGMENTS   *xiii*

INTRODUCTION   3

❧

PART ONE
Visions of Angels

RICHARD WILBUR   *Love Calls Us to the Things*   9
                        of This World

FRAY ANGELICO   *The Angel's New Wings*   10
  CHAVEZ

GENESIS 28:10–17   *Jacob's Dream of the Ladder*   21
                        to Heaven

ANONYMOUS   *Listen to the Angels Shouting*   22
                        (African-American Spiritual)

LUCILLE CLIFTON   *testament*   23

SOPHY BURNHAM   From *A Book of Angels*   24

DANTE	From *Purgatorio*	29
REVELATION 7:1-4, 7:9-12	*Sealing the Servants of God at the Last Judgment*	30
JOHN DONNE	*Holy Sonnet 7*	31
HOWARD FAST	*The General Zapped an Angel*	32
WALLACE STEVENS	*Angel Surrounded by Paysans*	44
MARIANNE MOORE	*By Disposition of Angels*	46

PART TWO

Talking with Angels

JACQUELINE OSCHEROW	*After Midnight, the Fifth Month*	49
EINAR KVARAN	*The Wish*	50
JAMES MERRILL	*A Dedication*	63
ALLAN GURGANUS	*It Had Wings*	63
REVELATION 10	*The Eating of the Little Scroll*	68
GENESIS 18:1-15	*Sarah's Laughter*	69
GENESIS 21:1-3	*Isaac's Birth*	70
PAMELA WHITE HADAS	*Mother and Other: seeing through laughter*	71
MARK TWAIN	From *Captain Stormfield's Visit to Heaven*	73

JOHN CHEEVER   *The Angel of the Bridge*   85

PHILIP SCHULTZ   *My Guardian Angel Stein*   97

PART THREE

Wrestling with Angels

JAMES MERRILL   *Angel*   103

FLANNERY O'CONNOR   *Letter to "A" from The Habit of Being*   104

GENESIS 32:24-32   *Jacob Wrestles with an Angel*   105

STEVE STERN   *Lazar Malkin Enters Heaven*   106

HAROLD BRODKEY   *From Angel*   120

LUCILLE CLIFTON   *to joan*   125

HOWARD SCHWARTZ   *The Evil Angel*   126

WILLIAM BUTLER YEATS   *The Mother of God*   129

LUCILLE CLIFTON   *mary's dream, holy night*   130
    island mary   131

THE KORAN   *Mary and Gabriel*   132

LOUISE ERDRICH   *The Visit*   133

ELIZABETH BARRETT BROWNING   *Sonnet XXII from Sonnets from the Portuguese*   134

VIRGINIA WOOLF   *From Professions for Women*   135

BILLY COLLINS   *Questions About Angels*   138

❦

PART FOUR

Angels in Difficulty

STEPHEN DUNN   *The Guardian Angel*   143

DONALD BARTHELME   *On Angels*   145

RUPERT BROOKE   *The Vision of the Archangels*   148

CLARICE LISPECTOR   *An Angel's Disquiet*   149

LEO TOLSTOY   *What Men Live By*   154

JAMES WRIGHT   *The Angel*   182

BERNARD MALAMUD   *Angel Levine*   185

A. R. AMMONS   *A Crippled Angel*   199

GABRIEL GARCÍA   *A Very Old Man with*   201
   MÁRQUEZ   *Enormous Wings*

❦

PART FIVE

Angels in the Landscape

WALLACE STEVENS   *Evening without Angels*   213

JOHN UPDIKE   *Archangel*   215

ELIZABETH BISHOP   *Seascape*   217

EUDORA WELTY   *A Still Moment*   218

VIRGINIA WOOLF	*Monday or Tuesday*	233
LESLIE ELLEN MOORE	*Herring Gulls: First Winter*	235
HERMAN MELVILLE	From *Moby Dick*	236
ANNE SEXTON	*Angel of Blizzards and Blackouts*	238
SYLVIA PLATH	*Black Rook in Rainy Weather*	239
FLANNERY O'CONNOR	*Revelation*	241
JACQUELINE OSCHEROW	*A Poem About Angels*	269

ACKNOWLEDGMENTS

I am grateful to all of the friends and colleagues who offered suggestions of angel stories and poems. I especially wish to thank Leslie Ellen Moore for her generous help in hammering out the shape of this book. Her lucidity and thoughtfulness have been a superb gift. I thank R. Clifton Spargo for his unusual fiction about angels and other figures, and for his inspiration. Peter Hawkins shared his bone-deep knowledge of Dante with me, and opened up questions about angels I had not thought to ask. Elizabeth Isele responded to an early version of my Introduction with perspicacity, grace, and care. Barbara Lassonde, my research assistant, became a true Angel of the Library, most necessary to me, and was constantly astonishing in her capacity to discover literature about angels. And I thank Lesley Malin Helm, my editor at Ballantine, for her honesty, humor, and insight. She has made my wrestling with angels a great pleasure indeed.

Closer to home, my children have given me rich encouragement, from the happy goad of Micah's perennial question, "So when is your angel book going to be here?" to the gift of an angel pin from Marissa, and the larger gift of her own growing capacity to write

XIV • *Literary Angels*

like an angel. Gabriel, although invisible through nine months of my work on this project, announced his presence through enthusiastic bumps and flutterings. Finally, I thank my husband Bryan Jay Wolf for his willingness to rub shoulders with angels for two years or more.

Literary Angels

Writing Like Angels

While collecting the poems and stories in this book, I often recalled the praise one of my teachers used to offer us, on rare and happy occasions: "You write like an angel." How do angels write? I imagined glorious creatures scrawling in midair with golden pens. What such figures write must be so magnificent, so transcendent, I thought, that the words would be difficult, maybe impossible, for human beings to read. A glimpse of a word here, half a sentence there, might be gleaned, only to fade from the sky and from memory like disappearing ink the following moment. How could such perfection be caught and held on earth?

Angels, however, have other things to do; they leave writing to mortals. Writing is a frustrating and joyous human act, one of the imperfect "things of this world" to which love calls us, as Richard Wilbur suggests in the opening poem of this book. Yet, while the act of writing is bound to the world, the words we write need not be. Words have an astonishing capacity, some days, to speed off the page and soar up into the air over our heads. To write like an angel, in this sense, is to encourage one's words to fly into extraordinary and unanticipated realms. When the subject one chooses is angels, such flights can be magnificent indeed. In the space of each poem or story included here, one can imagine a miraculous and divine world to be present and real.

I have been surprised by many of the angels in this collection. At first, I thought most of them would be as glorious as the familiar ones who float aloft in Renaissance splendor, with folds of white raiment and huge feathered wings, their heads in golden aureoles. I soon discovered that, although such resplendent figures could be found in some writings, the picture as a whole was richer and more complicated. I began to see how writers, at various times throughout the Judeo-Christian world, have presented remarkably different visions of such figures, and I started to chart these possibilities in the form of a story.

The story is not about angels all on their own, but rather the relationship between angels and people, sometimes quite ordinary people. Its movement resembles a love affair on a grand scale: the angels, first beheld from a distance as figures of divine splendor and significance, move earthward, to engage in ever more intricate relations with humans.

I have shaped this meeting of the angelic and the human into five parts. The first part, "Visions of Angels," contains the most visionary pieces, in which angels are figures of immense beauty and divine power, seen as signs or aspects of God. The respective writers feel amazement, awe, and confusion because it is nearly impossible to comprehend such extraordinary divinity and deep truth.

Such angels may appear human, yet most of them keep their distance in a magnificently ethereal realm. In the writings of the second section, "Talking with Angels," angels come down to earth to engage with people in more active and immediate ways. They often assume human form to guide, rescue, or warn those in need. Their power of speech can move human beings to new action. Those who receive angels in this section are open to the angels' words, and are often grateful. The angels know what they are talking about, and the people accept their whisperings and declarations, inspiration and advice with grace.

In the writings of the third section, "Wrestling with Angels," the relationship expands to include not only vision and language, as in the previous two sections, but touch—often an overwhelmingly intimate touch. As angels draw closer, the human response to such intimacy spans a rich spectrum, from teasing irritation to brooding, terror, or resistance. These more "real" angels are challenging and difficult. Yet, are such figures always to be trusted?

The penultimate section, "Angels in Difficulty," brings together stories and poems that reverse the situation of "wrestling with angels": these angels must wrestle with humans. To soar down from the heavens bringing love, knowledge, and divine aid is not always enough. These angels acknowledge their limitations; they may pity people, but they cannot prevent human death and sorrow. They shed their power and their simplicity to become as questioning and vulnerable as human beings. Human characters, far from receiving such angels with openness, often respond with coldness and unbearable cruelty. Yet the writers, in presenting these angels with compassion, offer another possibility: as angels become more human in nature, and more in need of our response, our love for these divine beings may increase.

In the concluding section, "Angels in the Landscape," angels have disappeared, in one sense, only to enter miraculously into the world, and into the act of writing itself. The human is now the angelic, and the capacity to see the divine in the ordinary, and to create something of beauty and significance out of an imperfect language, is a divine capacity.

The writers I have brought together in this book share the various powers of the angels they write about: they present us with visions; they give us messages, guide and rescue us; they overwhelm and provoke us; they afford us insight into the sorrows of others' lives, and of our own; and they show us the divine in the ordinary world. They do write like angels, and they invite us to put on our own wings, for the space of our reading, as we enter the rich landscapes of their words.

PART ONE

Visions of Angels

How do visions of angels surprise us? The writings in this section contain myriad possibilities: angels appear in dreams, or the heavens open up, out of the blue. Visions of angels sometimes enter into the texture of the ordinary: angels come with a rush and a rustle into a room, or show their magnificence dancing on a laundry line. These writers present themselves, or the figures they create, as witnesses of the divine. Such angels, in all their magnificence, signal the presence of God or the sacredness of the world. Yet how to describe what is divine? These accounts often strain at the bounds of words, attempting through language to gesture toward what cannot be brought into knowable form.

Love Calls Us to the Things of This World

RICHARD WILBUR

The eyes open to a cry of pulleys,
And spirited from sleep, the astounded soul
Hangs for a moment bodiless and simple
As false dawn.
                    Outside the open window
The morning air is all awash with angels.

Some are in bed-sheets, some are in blouses,
Some are in smocks: but truly there they are.
Now they are rising together in calm swells
Of halcyon feeling, filling whatever they wear
With the deep joy of their impersonal breathing;

Now they are flying in place, conveying
The terrible speed of their omnipresence, moving
And staying like white water; and now of a sudden
They swoon down into so rapt a quiet
That nobody seems to be there.
                    The soul shrinks

From all that it is about to remember,
From the punctual rape of every blessèd day,
And cries,
　　　　"Oh, let there be nothing on earth but laundry,
Nothing but rosy hands in the rising steam
And clear dances done in the sight of heaven."

　Yet, as the sun acknowledges
With a warm look the world's hunks and colors,
The soul descends once more in bitter love
To accept the waking body, saying now
In a changed voice as the man yawns and rises,

　"Bring them down from their ruddy gallows;
Let there be clean linen for the backs of thieves;
Let lovers go fresh and sweet to be undone,
And the heaviest nuns walk in a pure floating
Of dark habits,
　　　　keeping their difficult balance."

The Angel's New Wings

 FRAY ANGELICO CHAVEZ

Whiskery old Nabor blew over his flossy chin into the two holes he had finished gouging in the shoulders of a small wooden figure. Into one he stuck a newly whittled wing. It fitted loosely, but that could be fixed later with a sliver or two. He picked the other wing from his lap, pushed it into the second socket, and then stared into his empty hands!

No amount of painful peering under chair and table and bed disclosed the missing angel. The little fireplace of baked adobe in the corner held its single black pine-knot simmering on a heap of scarlet coals. The angel had simply vanished, slipped out of his hand the way sparrows or trout usually do, only much more swiftly.

From days unremembered Nabor Roybal had enjoyed the right of setting up the *nacimiento* in the old adobe church every time Christmas came to Rio Dormido. Not one living soul in Rio Dormido could recall when he as a youth had carved each figure out of pine. There was a smiling little Infant with a slim Mary to kneel at its side, and a Joseph who leaned drowsily on his staff; there were over a dozen shepherds in varied, stiff poses, and an unnumbered herd of sheep—folks said he added a sheep every year. An ox and an ass were the most true to life, everybody thought. And above all these hung an angel with outspread, stubby wings.

After the corn was brought in and husked, and the wheat or beans threshed by tiny black hoofs in the goat-corral, Nabor started to look forward to his beloved task. The first snow flurries creeping over the mesas surrounding the village told him that the great day drew nearer; and when the Padre wore deep penitential purple for Mass in the small but massive mud church of the Twelve Apostles, Nabor knew for sure that the Kingdom of God was at hand. Then it was high time to open his ancient carved chest of dovetailed boards where slept his *santos* in a welter of numberless wooden sheep.

But this year the harvest hustling, followed by a too early cold wave over the mesas, and also the final straws of old age, had forced Nabor to keep to his little room, its snug whitewashed comfort spoiled only by the inseparable aches in the old fellow's limbs and lungs. He could scarcely drag himself to the church the first Sunday the Padre put on purple. Christmas Eve found him unable to move from his little fireplace. Saddest of all, other hands were to set up the crib, for the first time since the little figures had been carved.

That afternoon Padre Arsenio sent some boys over to Nabor's house for the old chest with its quaint images. From that moment the traditions of generations began to be broken in various ways; for the priest had come back shortly afterward with one of the statues. There was a half-amused, half-pitying look on the young Padre's lean, dark face.

"Nabor, you must fix the angel for tonight," he had said. "The girl who was dusting the figures caught the wings with her rag and—"

The old man took the damaged seraph and squinted at it from odd angles before speaking. "I always thought the wings were too short anyway. My little Padre, soon I shall carve new ones, bigger and lighter ones."

"And one of the boys broke the burro's left fore-hoof," Padre Arsenio added, stepping astride the threshold. "But that can be hidden by the straw."

Shaking his white, shaggy head Nabor had opened his knife, reached for a piece of firewood and begun whittling. His mind limped back right away to the more even ground of the past, the time when he had shaped these little figures. Before that, as a boy, he had helped his father carve the corbels under the church rafters, and the twisted columns flanking the high reredos. Those days breathed reverence and faith. He recalled how both young and old kept a watch in the church on Christmas Eve before the midnight Mass, his father leading the singing of old Spanish carols. Those ancient traditions were slowly being broken—and now his dear little statues, too. Nabor thought all this aloud as he cut and blew, blew and whittled and scraped on bigger, better wings for the herald angel.

It was already dark when the Padre returned. This time his lean young face was far from amused. "Nabor," he panted, "all the images have been stolen!"

Nabor did not appear shocked by the news. He always looked stunned. After a silent span he asked with seeming calmness, "Who would want to steal them after all these years?"

"There are people in Santa Fé or Taos who buy them for good money, Nabor. Some good-for-nothing in Rio Dormido has run away with them for that purpose."

Nabor did not say anything more, did not even hear what the priest said after that. The Padre left him sitting on his chair by the fire, the two finished wings on his lap, and in one hand the little angel with two holes dug in its shoulders. Slowly, Nabor put in one wing, then the other—and the angel vanished.

·   ·   ·

A straight icy draught slicing the room's warmth made Nabor turn to the only window. On one of the four misty panes was a dark blotch, like the uneven outline of an angel flying. Nabor stuck his trembling hand through the dark spot, for the glass had been neatly cut out, or burned, or melted away. A few yards away from the window ran a fence of upright cedar posts, set close together like organ-pipes. Between two of these knotty palings was an opening of like shape. Brought into line, the hole in the window-light and the hole in the fence pointed like gunsights to the brightly lit front of the town dancehall.

The old man lost no time in looking for his coat and hat. The smart air outside gripped and shook his palsied frame, but not his purpose. Reeling and bobbing as though he had springs in his neck and under each shapeless shoe, Nabor reached the crowded *portal* of the dancehall.

Unnoticed by the men, who were intently watching two rolling, cursing brawlers on the porch floor, he touched a young fellow's elbow. "Boy," he stammered, "have you seen the angel? He flew straight this way." Had he been asking something more earthy, the youth might have returned his attention to the wrestlers. Instead he stared at Nabor.

"It was the angel of the crib," the old man explained further. "It had new wings, longer than the old ones."

The young man grinned wisely and gestured with a shrug. "Oh, yes, yes; it knocked off my sombrero when it flew into the hall."

Nabor thanked him and went in the doorway, only to be snatched into the swirl of crowded dancers, everybody ignoring him, pushing him and spinning him around from one couple to another. He was in the middle of the long room when the guitars and fiddles stopped, and someone called his name.

"Nabor, are you looking for a partner?"

"No, I am looking for an angel."

"That would be a wonderful partner for a polka or *la raspa*, old man. What sort of angel is she?"

"It is the angel of the crib, and his wings are newer than the old ones."

By this time many of the revelers had gathered around him. "Ah!" rang the voice of a laughing girl. "His wings are newer than the old ones! There he goes—up there!"

All eyes looked up with Nabor's at the rough rafters where a frightened sparrow flitted from one end of the hall to the other. The music started anew, and the dancers fell to milling around merrily. Once more Nabor was jostled about, until he staggered out of the hall's rear doorway. From across the deep-rutted lane, the brightly lighted windows of the village store shone into his face. A familiar dark outline on the large door pane drew him stumbling over the frost-hardened wheel-tracks.

The dark shape on the door-light turned out to be an eagle, pasted on the glass to advertise some brand of canned food. Inside, Nabor found himself in a maze of streamers trimmed with tinsel. A little Santa Claus, with a cotton beard whiter and longer than his own, seemed to greet him merrily. The fat storekeeper, who was weighing out some sugar with the added pressure of his thumb, called out to ask whether Nabor wanted something in a hurry.

"Did you see an angel fly through here? It was the angel of the crib, and he flew off when I put those new and larger wings on him."

The man behind the scales chuckled as he pulled out a silver dollar. "Friend Nabor, this is the only thing with wings that flies in here, and it flies out much faster."

Nabor shook his whiskers and shuffled outside in time to hear the whistling whirr of strong wings aloft somewhere behind the store. Supporting himself along the crooked adobe wall, he turned the rear corner and all but bumped into the dark shape of a man carrying a sack out of the storekeeper's corncrib. The prowler was about to drop his burden when he recognized the harmless intruder.

"Excuse me, *señor*," said the old man. "I just heard the angel fly behind this house. Did you see him?"

Before slipping away into the shadows, the man pointed mutely up at the dark sky. The silver shape of a startled pigeon wheeled about, like one of those tin lids that boys spin into the air, and came sailing back to the granary.

Nabor would have turned his steps homeward had not his eye caught the same bewitching outline on the goat-corral across the arroyo. Plainly stamped on the door of a shed on one side of the corral was the shape of wings and body, even a halo about the head. But the halo turned out to be only a knot-hole, and the rest a weather-mark on the rough planks.

Nevertheless, Nabor opened the door, which was slightly ajar, and went into the shed. The sharp, heaty scent of goats stung his nostrils as he paused to make sure if he had heard voices. A whisper, distinct in the smelly darkness, came to his ears. "Who can it be?" said a woman's voice; it was the storekeeper's wife, whom Nabor recognized.

"You people in there," he spoke softly, "have you seen an angel?"

A strange silence followed his query until Nabor explained: "It was the angel of the crib. When I fitted him with clean new wings he flew out of my hands."

"Yes, over there on the corner post," whispered the man, whose companion began to giggle. Nabor turned around to see a rooster which had flown up on a post and was cocking a curious head their way.

The goat-corral was the last structure on this side of Rio Dormido, and Nabor would have turned back had he not seen a silver flash on a large yellow pine that had long managed to thrive at the foot of the mesa not far away. Cries like those of a baby floated faintly down from the black needle-clusters. He was sure now that it was the angel—it moved up, down, up, against the lower part of the trunk. As he neared the tree a flock of frightened piñon jays flew away with babylike whimperings. But the angel still clung to the trunk, the way he used to hang upon the crib in the church. For Nabor, stumbling ever closer, the quest was ended.

Suddenly the thing stirred, tore itself backward from the rough bark, and flew with a soft, clapping noise to the mesa in measured downward swoops and upward jerks, like the flight of a flicker or any other kind of woodpecker. But that, too, would naturally be the flight of anything with wings of wood. Besides, did not his ears catch the wooden clapping? The thought put new strength in Nabor's legs as he began to climb toward the bleak rim of the mesa sharply lined against a hazily moonlit sky.

It was not moonlight, however, that lit the higher terrain, Nabor soon found out. As his head rose above the low palisade of tufa boulders, he stood frozen in his tracks to see a little figure hovering a few feet above the tableland. It was bathed in an unearthly glow. Its body was the same age-worn figure in faded colors which he had so often caressed with rough but loving fingers. Its wings were fresh, unpainted firewood, and they moved a little, like those of a soaring hawk, for Nabor had not had time to fasten them tightly with tiny pegs. He could even hear them squeak in their sockets.

And there were shepherds watching, his own little shepherds in stiff poses, with surprised faces, *and keeping the night watches over their flocks*—his own little sheep that sprawled half-hidden all over the dried prairie grass.

And the angel said to them: "Fear not, for this day is born to you a Saviour, Who is Christ the Lord, in the city of David. And this shall be a sign to you. You shall find the Infant wrapped in swaddling clothes, and laid in a manger."

And suddenly there was with the angel a multitude of the heavenly army, being of the same size as the angel but not of wood, *praising God and saying: "Glory to God in the highest, and on earth peace to men of good will."*

With this the sprite-like chorus vanished, and the angel of the crib swept down to the village of adobe with the jerky swoops of a flicker, while the aroused shepherds began to round up their flocks and drive them down the edge of the mesa.

. . .

Nabor hurried back to Rio Dormido, past the silent pine and goat-corral, past the now darkened store and dancehall, and into the dimly lit church of the Twelve Apostles. The Padre was already intoning the *Gloria* at the candle-banked altar. Nabor strode shakily between the rows of worshipers, unaware of the knowing glances and smiles which they exchanged among themselves, for his rheumy gaze was fixed on the empty crib far in front near the altar. A flutter of wings among the carved *vigas* and corbels above made everybody look up. The people saw a bewildered sparrow. But Nabor saw a little angel of wood which sailed down to the crib and with a soft click and a clump hooked himself at his wonted place above the crib.

As the old man knelt down, the rear wall of the crib shook

somewhat, and through the open gate shuffled an ox over the straw. The animal doubled its forelegs, rolled over on its side, and regarded Nabor with swaying jaws. Then came an old man with a staff leading a limping burro on which rode a pretty maiden. Nabor felt sorry for the donkey, which winced each time its hoofless stump touched the ground. Tenderly Joseph lifted the kneeling woman from the donkey's back; gently he laid her on a pile of straw; and there she lay in quiet, as though she were wholly spent from a long journey, her knees drawn up as she had been carved long ago.

By and by Padre Arsenio sang the *Credo*, and when the choir came to the words, *"Et incarnatus est de Spiritu Sancto ex Maria Virgine,"* the people in the nave knelt down with much noise. Right away Mary woke and raised herself in her kneeling posture on the straw. Now Nabor noticed with wonder that the statue, whose slim waist he had carved with delicate touch while turning tender *Aves* on his tongue, was seemingly great. And whilst his eyes wondered, his ear caught a low noise, like the scraping of a knife on a stick. It was Joseph, leaning on his staff, and snoring softly.

The bell of Consecration woke neither Mary from her rapture nor Joseph from his slumber. For a brief spell, when the priest raised aloft the Host, and then the Chalice, Nabor had turned to the altar. As he peered back into the crib he found Mary, now maidenly slim as he had carved her, kneeling beside the manger. Joseph, too, stood staring down over his staff at the little wooden Child that smiled at them from the straw. And immediately the rear wall began to quake as droves of sheep rushed in, as sheep will do, crushing each other in a shouldering pack. They sprawled all about, some even crawling under the manger, as the panting shepherds followed after with expressions of awe and joy.

Later, the bell at the altar tinkled again. Nabor left the crib for the first time with anxious backward glances, and stumbled to the Communion railing, where men, women, and children were elbowing each other for a place. Nabor could not hold himself in the meantime from looking back at the nave. At a glance he saw the woman of the goat-corral, drowsily swinging her rosary beads from her fingers; beside her sat her sleepyeyed husband, the fat storekeeper. Behind her were the women and girls who had pushed him around the dancehall floor; of their male companions, some leaned lazily against the walls, others stood idly about the blazing stove.

When Nabor returned and knelt once more before the *nacimiento*, he noticed to his dismay that the shepherds with their flocks were already gone. He had no time to wonder before he heard a faint click. The angel had unhooked itself and had dropped lightly at Joseph's side, whispering something into his ear. Nabor drew closer. *"Arise,"* said the angel, *"and take the Child and His mother, and fly into Egypt; and be there until I shall tell thee. For it will come to pass that Herod will seek the Child to destroy Him."* Thus saying, the angel flitted back to his hook.

Mary grasped the Child to her breast, and Joseph lifted them both onto the burro's back. Joseph led it out limping under its sweet swaying burden, leaving the gate open behind them. Nabor knelt there overcome by the rise of dismay in his breast, gazing reproachfully at the ox, which glared back at him chewing its cud. At last the beast rolled back to its knees, stood up with an effort, and it too went out with slow, shuffling gait.

• • •

The people were all gone when Padre Arsenio came back from the sacristy wrapped in his woolen cloak. He did not see the trembling old man crouched at the crib until he had turned from barring the front doors with a heavy beam and from snuffing out the paraffin candles in their tin sconces along the walls.

"So you had to come to the midnight Mass, Nabor?" the Padre spoke, raising him up from the cold floor. "We missed the adoration of the Child this year. I am very sorry the images were stolen."

Nabor's eyes regarded the Padre's with bewilderment. Perhaps the young cleric was somewhat touched in the head, like the rest of the world. The thought in Father Arsenio's mind was that Nabor was at the end of his days, mentally as well as bodily. Sharing part of his mantle with the stooped, ragged shoulders, he led the old man to his rooms for a sip of hot coffee or wine. As he blew out the last candles by the side door, darkness swallowed up the corbels, the reredos, the empty crib and the lonely angel with its new wings.

Jacob's Dream of the Ladder to Heaven

 GENESIS 28:10–17

Jacob left Beer-sheba, and went toward Haran. And he came to a certain place, and stayed there that night, because the sun had set. Taking one of the stones of the place, he put it under his head and lay down in that place to sleep. And he dreamed that there was a ladder set up on the earth, and the top of it reached to heaven; and behold, the angels of God were ascending and descending on it!

And behold, the Lord stood above it and said, "I am the Lord, the God of Abraham your father and the God of Isaac; the land on which you lie I will give to you and to your descendants; and your descendants shall be like the dust of the earth, and you shall spread abroad to the west and to the east and to the north and to the south; and by you and your descendants shall all the families of the earth bless themselves. Behold, I am with you and will keep you wherever you go, and will bring you back to this land; for I will not leave you until I have done that of which I have spoken to you." Then Jacob awoke from his sleep and said, "Surely the Lord is in this place; and I did not know it."

And he was afraid, and said, "How awesome is this place! This is none other than the house of God, and this is the gate of heaven."

Listen to the Angels Shouting

(AFRICAN–AMERICAN SPIRITUAL)

Where do you think I found my soul?
    Listen to the angels shouting.
I found my soul at Hell's dark door.
    Listen to the angels shouting.
Before I lie in Hell one day
    (Listen to the angels shouting),
I sing and pray my soul away
    (Listen to the angels shouting).

I don't know what sinners want to stay here for.
 Listen to the angels shouting.
When he gets home he'll sorrow no more.
 Listen to the angels shouting.

Run all the way,
Run all the way,
Run all the way, my Lord.
Listen to the angels shouting.

Blow, Gabriel, blow,
Blow, Gabriel, blow.
Tell all the joyful news.
Listen to the angels shouting.

Brethren will you come to the promised land?
 Listen to the angels shouting.
Come and sing with the heavenly band.
 Listen to the angels shouting.

testament

 LUCILLE CLIFTON

in the beginning
 was the word.

the year of our lord,
amen. i
lucille clifton
hereby testify
that in that room
there was a light
and in that light
there was a voice
and in that voice
there was a sigh
and in that sigh
there was a world.
a world a sigh a voice a light and
i
alone
in a room.

From *A Book of Angels*

SOPHY BURNHAM

When I saw the angel, I didn't go to church, and neither do I remember praying very much. I was twenty-eight. My husband was a writer for *The CBS Evening News with Walter Cronkite*, and we lived in Greenwich Village, in a fifth-floor walk-up, struggling. I had left a career to follow David to New York. We had just had our first baby, and suddenly I found myself trapped in an apartment with an infant entirely dependent on me, who could not talk or give back either emotional or physical help. How did I manage? There were days when I could easily imagine picking up the baby by the heels and smashing her head against the bare brick wall. . . . I wept a lot. During the day I dared not leave her alone. At night, when David came home, the streets were said to be too dangerous for me to go out walking all alone. I was a prisoner.

I found part-time work. I wrote. The baby grew bigger. I grew stronger. My attention was hardly directed to the mysterious, therefore. I was struggling with practical realities—doubt, confusion, suffering.

One day a friend telephoned asking if David and I would join a party of his friends for a week of skiing in Val d'Isère in France. We agreed. We left the baby, eight months old, with my mother, and found a charter flight to France.

We were both good skiers. We had spent time learning it with the discipline and concentration that we brought to most of the things we did. In addition I found in skiing something so pure and fine it lifted me beyond myself. Riding a single chairlift, swinging in the silence of the winds, and blinking against the ice-encrusted trees, prisms glittering against a hard blue sky, my body taut and fit; I thought that nothing could match the crack of such sensations. Fast and fearless, I shot downhill, fell, rose, and plunged on in that cold white air.

Just once when skiing I had seen something else.

When we were newly married, we'd gone skiing in Austria. We joined a class and were toiling across a difficult slope on a long up-hill traverse, when I looked up and saw the sky flaming with color.

"Look! Look at the sky!" I pointed, dumbfounded by the shimmering pinks and greens, colors I had never seen in sky before. Our guide and David and the class looked up and then away, as if it were of no significance. Didn't they see it? Or was I sun-dazzled—overworked perhaps—so that I only imagined this effect?

"Yes, we often have interesting phenomena in the mountains," said the instructor, and continued with his class. Continue the lesson! I was riveted to that blazing sky.

I did not remember that sky again until I saw it for a second time, in Val d'Isère.

At Val d'Isère you feel you're standing at the top of the world. High above the treeline lie white fields of snow. Sometimes you ski in clouds. Sometimes the air is clear as the stratosphere. You ski on tracks, or *pistes*. These are marked by an occasional red flag stuck in the snow. But mostly you know where to go by the tracks of other skiers, and you do not leave the paths. There are two reasons. First, you can plunge off a cliff, and second, you can start an avalanche. There is no ski patrol at Val d'Isère to sweep the trails at night for injured skiers as there are in low-lying mountains like Stowe, Vermont, or Aspen, Colorado. At least there wasn't a ski patrol then.

One day our party skied to Tignes. It is a full day's trip, up the funicular to a high peak, then one long run that takes most of the morning and ends in a nearby town. In the afternoon you ski at Tignes and take a bus back home.

It had not snowed for weeks. The track was packed hard as a toboggan slide. I came fast around one curve and just at the edge of the path, I fell, and found myself sliding on my back head first, downhill. When you fall skiing, you're supposed to twist your skis around to the downhill side, dig into the snow, and brake to a stop. No matter how I tried, I could not make that twist. The ground was hard and somewhat pebbly. It acted like a billion ball bearings, carrying me along. I remember thinking it was ludicrous, sledding on my back, headfirst, battered against small stones. I was not afraid, though I knew I was off the *piste*. After two or three attempts, however, to flip my skis, I decided it didn't matter, that soon I would hit a tree—no, I meant a rock—and stop.

For my attention was captured by the sky. The sky! It wasn't just blue sky. It radiated blue, green, yellow, pink; and my heart was wrenched out of my body with rapture as if it recognized something—*Home!* I was barreling downhill at thirty or forty miles an hour, bumping over stones, yet filled with joy. I saw the perfection of all things, including this mad, headfirst slide. What did it matter if I died right then? I thought irrationally. That, too, was welcome. Wondrous.

Suddenly a blur of black—and I piled into another skier's legs.

David, at the top of the slope, saw what happened as he stood there wondering what to do. He told me later how a man shot past him, "out of nowhere," as he said, skiing like crazy. He tore down the slope, a bullet winging past me, then turned and dug in his skis. I fell against his legs. It didn't hurt. Neither did he fall with the impact or even apparently stumble and have to catch his weight as one-hundred-twenty pounds plowed into him at such high speed.

I stood up. He was dressed completely in black: black hat, black parka, black pants, black skis. This was strange, because no one dressed in black on the ski slopes then, but in vibrant yellows, reds, and blues.

"*Merci beaucoup,*" I said. Then I looked into his eyes. They, too, were black, but full of such light I could not move.

"*Merci,*" I said again. I do not remember his answering. I don't remember any voice. He turned and started up the hill, herringboning, but at such speed! He had the strength of giants. Each of his steps counted for two or three of mine, though I could keep up with any skier I'd ever met before. I clambered after him, hurrying, pushing myself. I wanted to look into his eyes again. I wanted to ask him who he was and hear his voice, though these were not developed thoughts, but merely the propelling force. At the top he took off immediately, ignoring David, who reached out likewise to thank him. He zoomed away. A minute later I reached the top. David caught me. "Are you all right?" But I pushed away. "Yes, yes," I called as I raced down the track after the man in black, who had already disappeared around the curve of the hill.

The path here was wide and steep. It plunged downhill, curved to the left around an outcropping of rocks, and opened to a vista of the whole valley below—mile upon mile of open space.

No one was in sight.

I came past the rocks, casting right and left, looking for a pocket in which he could have disappeared. The only people in sight were tiny specks far down the valley in Tignes, black dots. It was inconceivable that he could have shot the valley walls that fast. Yet he had disappeared.

I skied on. Partway down the mountain my stomach dropped. To my left rose a cliff. It was at the top of this that I had fallen. Had I not been stopped, I would have fallen off the cliff to a rubble of rocks below. Only that skier had stopped me from being killed.

We skied to the valley floor, David and I, stopped for refreshments, and took small runs on the T-bars and Poma lifts until it was time to take the bus back to Val d'Isère. Everywhere I went I looked for that man, so easily identifiable in black. I told myself it was only because I wanted to thank him properly, but on the bus ride back to Val d'Isère I stared out the black window at the darkened countryside, lost in the memory of those eyes.

For the next week I looked for him. I never saw him again.

From *Purgatorio*

 DANTE

    And just as Mars, when it is overcome
by the invading mists of dawn, glows red
above the waters' plain, low in the west,
    so there appeared to me—and may I see it
again—a light that crossed the sea: so swift,
there is no flight of bird to equal it.
    When, for a moment, I'd withdrawn my eyes
that I might ask a question of my guide,
I saw that light again, larger, more bright.
    Then, to each side of it, I saw a whiteness,
though I did not know what the whiteness was;
below, another whiteness slowly showed.
    My master did not say a word before
the whitenesses first seen appeared as wings;
but then, when he had recognized the helmsman,
    he cried: "Bend, bend your knees: behold the angel
of God, and join your hands; from this point on,
this is the kind of minister you'll meet.

See how much scorn he has for human means;
he'd have no other sail than his own wings
and use no oar between such distant shores.

See how he holds his wings, pointing to Heaven,
piercing the air with his eternal pinions,
which do not change as mortal plumage does."

Then he—that bird divine—as he drew closer
and closer to us, seemed to gain in brightness,
so that my eyes could not endure his nearness,

and I was forced to lower them; and he
came on to shore with boat so light, so quick
that nowhere did the water swallow it.

Sealing the Servants of God at the Last Judgment

REVELATION 7:1–4, 7:9–12

After this I saw four angels standing at the four corners of the
earth, holding back the four winds of the earth, that no wind might
blow on earth or sea or against any tree. Then I saw another angel
ascend from the rising of the sun, with the seal of the living God,
and he called with a loud voice to the four angels who had been
given power to harm earth and sea, saying, "Do not harm the earth
or the sea or the trees, till we have sealed the servants of our God
upon their foreheads." And I heard the number of the sealed, a hundred and forty-four thousand sealed, out of every tribe of the sons
of Israel.

• • •

After this I looked, and behold, a great multitude which no man could number, from every nation, from all tribes and peoples and tongues, standing before the throne and before the Lamb, clothed in white robes, with palm branches in their hands, and crying out with a loud voice, "Salvation belongs to our God who sits upon the throne, and to the Lamb!" And all the angels stood round the throne and round the elders and the four living creatures, and they fell on their faces before the throne and worshiped God, saying, "Amen! Blessing and glory and wisdom and thanksgiving and honor and power and might be to our God for ever and ever! Amen."

Holy Sonnet 7

 JOHN DONNE

At the round earth's imagined corners, blow
Your trumpets, angels, and arise, arise
From death, you numberless infinities
Of souls, and to your scattered bodies go,
All whom the flood did, and fire shall o'erthrow,
All whom war, dearth, age, agues, tyrannies,
Despair, law, chance, hath slain, and you whose eyes,
Shall behold God, and never taste death's woe.
But let them sleep, Lord, and me mourn a space,

For, if above all these, my sins abound,
'Tis late to ask abundance of thy grace,
When we are there; here on this lowly ground,
Teach me how to repent; for that's as good
As if thou hadst sealed my pardon, with thy blood.

The General Zapped an Angel

HOWARD FAST

When news leaked out of Viet Nam that Old Hell and Hardtack Mackenzie had shot down an angel, every newspaper in the world dug into its morgue for the background and biography of this hard-bitten old warrior.

Not that General Clayborne Mackenzie was so old. He had only just passed his fiftieth birthday, and he had plenty of piss and vinegar left in him when he went out to Viet Nam to head up the 55th Cavalry and its two hundred helicopters; and the sight of him sitting in the open door of a gunship, handling a submachine gun like the pro he was, and zapping anything that moved there below—because anything that moved was likely enough to be Charlie—had inspired many a fine color story.

Correspondents liked to stress the fact that Mackenzie was a "natural fighting man," with, as they put it, "an instinct for the kill." In this they were quite right, as the material from the various newspaper morgues proved. When Mackenzie was only six years old, playing in the yard of his humble North Carolina home, he managed to kill a puppy by beating it to death with a stone, an extraordinary act of courage and perseverance. After that, he was able to earn spending money by killing unwanted puppies and kittens for five cents each. He was an intensely creative child, one of the things that contributed to his subsequent leadership qualities, and not content with drowning the animals, he devised five other methods for destroying the unwanted pets. By nine he was trapping rabbits and rats and had invented a unique yet simple mole trap that caught moles alive. He enjoyed turning over live moles and mice to neighborhood cats, and often he would invite his little playmates to watch the results. At the age of twelve his father gave him his first gun—and from there on no one who knew young Clayborne Mackenzie doubted either his future career or success.

After his arrival in Viet Nam, there was no major mission of the 55th that Old Hell and Hardtack did not lead in person. The sight of him blazing away from the gunship became a symbol of the "new war," and the troops on the ground would look for him and up at him and cheer him when he appeared. (Sometimes the cheers were earthy, but that is only to be expected in war.) There was nothing Mackenzie loved better than a village full of skulking, treacherous VC, and once he passed over such a village, little was left of it. A young newspaper correspondent compared him to an "avenging angel," and sometimes when his helicopters were called in to help a group of hard-pressed infantry, he thought of himself in such terms. It was on just such an occasion, when the company of marines holding the outpost at Quen-to were so hard pressed, that the thing happened.

General Clayborne Mackenzie had led the attack, blazing away, and down came the angel, square into the marine encampment. It took a while for them to realize what they had, and Mackenzie had already returned to base field when the call came from Captain Joe Kelly, who was in command of the marine unit.

"General, sir," said Captain Kelly, when Mackenzie had picked up the phone and asked what in hell they wanted, "General Mackenzie, sir, it would seem that you shot down an angel."

"Say that again, Captain."

"An angel, sir."

"A what?"

"An angel, sir."

"And just what in hell is an angel?"

"Well," Kelly answered. "I don't quite know how to answer that, sir. An angel is an angel. One of God's angels, sir."

"Are you out of your goddamn mind, Captain?" Mackenzie roared. "Or are you sucking pot again? So help me God, I warned you potheads that if you didn't lay off the grass I would see you all in hell!"

"No, sir," said Kelly quietly and stubbornly. "We have no pot here."

"Well put on Lieutenant Garcia!" Mackenzie yelled.

"Lieutenant Garcia." The voice came meekly.

"Lieutenant, what the hell is this about an angel?"

"Yes, General."

"Yes, what?"

"It is an angel. When you were over here zapping VC—well, sir, you just went and zapped an angel."

"So help me God," Mackenzie yelled, "I will break every one of you potheads for this! You got a lot of guts, buster, to put on a full general, but nobody puts me on and walks away from it. Just remember that."

One thing about Old Hell and Hardtack, when he wanted something done, he didn't ask for volunteers. He did it himself, and now he went to his helicopter and told Captain Jerry Gates, the pilot:

"You take me out to that marine encampment at Quen-to and put me right down in the middle of it."

"It's a risky business, General."

"It's your goddamn business to fly this goddamn ship and not to advise me."

Twenty minutes later the helicopter settled down into the encampment at Quen-to, and a stony-faced full general faced Captain Kelly and said:

"Now suppose you just lead me to that damn angel, and God help you if it's not."

But it was; twenty feet long and all of it angel, head to foot. The marines had covered it over with two tarps, and it was their good luck that the VCs either had given up on Quen-to or had simply decided not to fight for a while—because there was not much fight left in the marines, and all the young men could do was to lie in their holes and try not to look at the big body under the two tarps and not to talk about it either; but in spite of how they tried, they kept sneaking glances at it and they kept on whispering about it, and the two of them who pulled off the tarps so that General Mackenzie might see began to cry a little. The general didn't like that; if there was one thing he did not like, it was soldiers who cried, and he snapped at Kelly:

"Get these two mothers the hell out of here, and when you assign a detail to me, I want men, not wet-nosed kids." Then he surveyed the angel, and even he was impressed.

"It's a big son of a bitch, isn't it?"

"Yes, sir. Head to heel, it's twenty feet. We measured it."

"What makes you think it's an angel?"

"Well, that's the way it is," Kelly said. "It's an angel. What else is it?"

General Mackenzie walked around the recumbent form and had to admit the logic in Captain Kelly's thinking. The thing was white, not flesh-white but snow-white, shaped like a man, naked, and sprawled on its side with two great feathered wings folded under it. Its hair was spun gold and its face was too beautiful to be human.

"So that's an angel," Mackenzie said finally.

"Yes, sir."

"Like hell it is!" Mackenzie snorted. "What I see is a white, Caucasian male, dead of wounds suffered on the field of combat. By the way, where'd I hit him?"

"We can't find the wounds, sir."

"Now just what the hell do you mean, you can't find the wounds? I don't miss. If I shot it, I shot it."

"Yes, sir. But we can't find the wounds. Perhaps its skin is very tough. It might have been the concussion that knocked it down."

Used to getting at the truth of things himself, Mackenzie walked up and down the body, going over it carefully. No wounds were visible.

"Turn the angel over," Mackenzie said.

Kelly, who was a good Catholic, hesitated at first; but between a live general and a dead angel, the choice was specified. He called out a detail of marines, and without enthusiasm they managed to turn over the giant body. When Mackenzie complained that mud smears were impairing his inspection, they wiped the angel clean. There were no wounds on the other side either.

"That's a hell of a note," Mackenzie muttered, and if Captain Kelly and Lieutenant Garcia had been more familiar with the moods of Old Hell and Hardtack, they would have heard a tremor of uncertainty in his voice. The truth is that Mackenzie was just a little baffled. "Anyway," he decided, "it's dead, so wrap it up and put it in the ship."

"Sir?"

"God damn it, Kelly, how many times do I have to give you an order? I said, wrap it up and put it in the ship!"

The marines at Quen-to were relieved as they watched Mackenzie's gunship disappear in the distance, preferring the company of live VCs to that of a dead angel, but the pilot of the helicopter flew with all the assorted worries of a Southern Fundamentalist.

"Is that sure enough an angel, sir?" he had asked the general.

"You mind your eggs and fly the ship, son," the general replied. An hour ago he would have told the pilot to keep his goddamn nose out of things that didn't concern him, but the angel had a stultifying effect on the general's language. It depressed him, and when the three-star general at headquarters said to him, "Are you trying to tell me, Mackenzie, that you shot down an angel?" Mackenzie could only nod his head miserably.

"Well, sir, you are out of your goddamn mind."

"The body's outside in Hangar F," said Mackenzie. "I put a guard over it, sir."

The two-star general followed the three-star general as he stalked to Hangar F, where the three-star general looked at the body, poked it with his toe, poked it with his finger, felt the feathers, felt the hair, and then said:

"God damn it to hell, Mackenzie, do you know what you got here?"

"Yes, sir."

"You got an angel—that's what the hell you got here."

"Yes, sir, that's the way it would seem."

"God damn you, Mackenzie, I always had a feeling that I should have put my foot down instead of letting you zoom up and down out there in those gunships zapping VCs. My God almighty, you're supposed to be a grown man with some sense instead of some dumb kid who wants to make a score zapping Charlie, and if you hadn't been out there in that gunship this would never have happened. Now what in hell am I supposed to do? We got a lousy enough press on this war. How am I going to explain a dead angel?"

"Maybe we don't explain it, sir. I mean, there it is. It happened. The damn thing's dead, isn't it? Let's bury it. Isn't that what a soldier does—buries his dead, tightens his belt a notch, and goes on from there?"

"So we bury it, huh, Mackenzie?"

"Yes, sir. We bury it."

"You're a horse's ass, Mackenzie. How long since someone told you that? That's the trouble with being a general in this goddamn army—no one ever gets to tell you what a horse's ass you are. You got dignity."

"No, sir. You're not being fair, sir," Mackenzie protested. "I'm trying to help. I'm trying to be creative in this trying situation."

"You get a gold star for being creative, Mackenzie. Yes, sir, General—that's what you get. Every marine at Quen-to knows you shot down an angel. Your helicopter pilot and crew know it, which means that by now everyone on this base knows it—because anything that happens here, I know it last—and those snotnose reporters on the base, they know it, not to mention the goddamn chaplains, and you want to bury it. Bless your heart."

The three-star general's name was Drummond, and when he got back to his office, his aide said to him excitedly:

"General Drummond, sir, there's a committee of chaplains, sir, who insist on seeing you, and they're very uptight about something, and I know how you feel about chaplains, but this seems to be something special, and I think you ought to see them."

"I'll see them." General Drummond sighed.

There were four chaplains, a Catholic priest, a rabbi, an Episcopalian, and a Lutheran. The Methodist, Baptist, and Presbyterian chaplains had wanted to be a part of the delegation, but the priest, who was a Paulist, said that if they were to bring in five Protestants, he wanted a Jesuit as reenforcement, while the rabbi, who was Reform, agreed that against five Protestants an Orthodox rabbi ought to join the Jesuit. The result was a compromise, and they agreed to allow the priest, Father Peter O'Malley, to talk for the group. Father O'Malley came directly to the point:

"Our information is, General, that General Mackenzie has shot down one of God's holy angels. Is that or is that not so?"

"I'm afraid it's so," Drummond admitted.

There was a long moment of silence while the collective clergy gathered its wits, its faith, its courage, and its astonishment, and then Father O'Malley asked slowly and ominously:

"And what have you done with the body of this holy creature, if indeed it has a body?"

"It has a body—a very substantial body. In fact, it's as large as a young elephant, twenty feet tall. It's lying in Hangar F, under guard."

Father O'Malley shook his head in horror, looked at his Protestant colleagues, and then passed over them to the rabbi and said to him:

"What are your thoughts, Rabbi Bernstein?"

Since Rabbi Bernstein represented the oldest faith that was concerned with angels, the others deferred to him.

"I think we ought to look upon it immediately," the rabbi said.

"I agree," said Father O'Malley.

The other clergy joined in this agreement, and they repaired to Hangar F, a journey not without difficulty, for by now the press had come to focus on the story, and the general and the clergy ran a sort of gauntlet of pleading questions as they made their way on foot to Hangar F. The guards there barred the press, and the clergy entered with General Drummond and General Mackenzie and a half a dozen other staff officers. The angel was uncovered, and the men made a circle around the great, beautiful thing, and then for almost five minutes there was silence.

Father O'Malley broke the silence. "God forgive us," he said.

There was a circle of amens, and then more silence, and finally Whitcomb, the Episcopalian, said:

"It could conceivably be a natural phenomenon."

Father O'Malley looked at him wordlessly, and Rabbi Bernstein softened the blow with the observation that even God and His holy angels could be considered as not apart from nature, whereupon Pastor Yager, the Lutheran, objected to a pantheistic viewpoint at a time like this, and Father O'Malley snapped:

"The devil with this theological nonsense! The plain fact of the matter is that we are standing in front of one of God's holy angels, which we in our animal-like sinfulness have slain. What penance we must do is more to the point."

"Penance is your field, gentlemen," said General Drummond. "I have the problem of a war, the press, and this body."

"This body, as you call it," said Father O'Malley, "obviously should be sent to the Vatican—immediately, if you ask me."

"Oh, ho!" snorted Whitcomb. "The Vatican! No discussion, no exchange of opinion—oh, no, just ship it off to the Vatican where it can be hidden in some secret dungeon with any other evidence of God's divine favor—"

"Come now, come now," said Rabbi Bernstein soothingly. "We are witness to something very great and holy, and we should not argue as to where this holy thing of God belongs. I think it is obvious that it belongs in Jerusalem."

While this theological discussion raged, it occurred to General Clayborn Mackenzie that his own bridges needed mending, and he stepped outside to where the press—swollen by now to almost the entire press corps in Viet Nam—waited; and of course they grabbed him.

"Is it true, General?"

"Is what true?"

"Did you shoot down an angel?"

"Yes, I did," the old warrior stated forthrightly.

"For heaven's sake, why?" asked a woman photographer.

"It was a mistake," said Old Hell and Hardtack modestly.

"You mean you didn't see it?" asked another voice.

"No, sir. Peripheral, if you know what I mean. I was in the gunship zapping Charlie, and bang—there it was."

The press was skeptical. A dozen questions came, all to the point of how he knew that it was an angel.

"You don't ask why a river's a river or a donkey's a donkey," Mackenzie said bluntly. "Anyway, we have professional opinion inside."

Inside, the professional opinion was divided and angry. All were agreed that the angel was a sign—but what kind of sign was another matter entirely. Pastor Yager held that it was a sign for peace, calling for an immediate cease-fire. Whitcomb, the Episcopalian, held, however, that it was merely a condemnation of indiscriminate zapping, while the rabbi and the priest held that it was a sign—period. Drummond said that sooner or later the press must be allowed in and that the network men must be permitted to put the dead angel on television. Whitcomb and the rabbi agreed. O'Malley and Yager demurred. General Robert L. Robert of the Engineer Corps arrived with secret information that the whole thing was a put-on by the Russians and that the angel was a robot, but when they attempted to cut the flesh to see whether the angel bled or not, the skin proved to be impenetrable.

At that moment the angel stirred, just a trifle, yet enough to make the clergy and brass gathered around him leap back to give him room—for that gigantic twenty-foot form, weighing better than half a ton, was one thing dead and something else entirely alive. The angel's biceps were as thick around as a man's body, and his great, beautiful head was mounted on a neck almost two feet in diameter. Even the clerics were sufficiently hazy on angelology to be at all certain that even an angel might not resent being shot down. As he stirred a second time, the men around him moved even farther away, and some of the brass nervously loosened their sidearms.

"If this holy creature is alive," Rabbi Bernstein said bravely, "then he will have neither hate nor anger toward us. His nature is of love and forgiveness. Don't you agree with me, Father O'Malley?"

If only because the Protestant ministers were visibly dubious, Father O'Malley agreed. "By all means. Oh, yes."

"Just how the hell do you know?" demanded General Drummond, loosening his sidearm. "That thing has the strength of a bulldozer."

Not to be outdone by a combination of Catholic and Jew, Whitcomb stepped forward bravely and faced Drummond and said, "That 'thing,' as you call it, sir, is one of the Almighty's blessed angels, and you would do better to see to your immortal soul than to your sidearm."

To which Drummond yelled, "Just who the hell do you think you are talking to, mister—just—"

At that moment the angel sat up, and the men around him leaped away to widen the circle. Several drew their sidearms; others whispered whatever prayers they could remember. The angel, whose eyes were as blue as the skies over Viet Nam when the monsoon is gone and the sun shines through the washed air, paid almost no attention to them at first. He opened one wing and then the other, and his great wings almost filled the hangar. He flexed one arm and then the other, and then he stood up.

On his feet, he glanced around him, his blue eyes moving steadily from one to another, and when he did not find what he sought, he walked to the great sliding doors of Hangar F and spread them open with a single motion. To the snapping of steel regulators and the grinding of stripped gears, the doors parted—revealing to the crowd outside, newsmen, officers, soldiers, and civilians, the mighty, twenty-foot-high, shining form of the angel.

No one moved. The sight of the angel, bent forward slightly, his splendid wings half spread, not for flight but to balance him, held them hypnotically fixed, and the angel himself moved his eyes from face to face, finding finally what he sought—none other than Old Hell and Hardtack Mackenzie.

As in those Western films where the moment of "truth," as they call it, is at hand, where sheriff and badman stand face to face, their hands twitching over their guns—as the crowd melts away from the two marked men in those films, so did the crowd melt away from around Mackenzie until he stood alone—as alone as any man on earth.

The angel took a long, hard look at Mackenzie, and then the angel sighed and shook his head. The crowd parted for him as he walked past Mackenzie and down the field—where, squarely in the middle of Runway Number 1, he spread his mighty wings and took off, the way an eagle leaps from his perch into the sky, or—as some reporters put it—as a dove flies gently.

Angel Surrounded by Paysans

 WALLACE STEVENS

One of the countrymen:

There is
A welcome at the door to which no one comes?

The angel:
    I am the angel of reality,
    Seen for a moment standing in the door.

    I have neither ashen wing nor wear of ore
    And live without a tepid aureole,

    Or stars that follow me, not to attend,
    But, of my being and its knowing, part.

    I am one of you and being one of you
    Is being and knowing what I am and know.

    Yet I am the necessary angel of earth,
    Since, in my sight, you see the earth again,

    Cleared of its stiff and stubborn, man-locked set,
    And, in my hearing, you hear its tragic drone

    Rise liquidly in liquid lingerings,
    Like watery words awash; like meanings said

    By repetitions of half-meanings. Am I not,
    Myself, only half of a figure of a sort,

    A figure half seen, or seen for a moment, a man
    Of the mind, an apparition apparelled in

Apparels of such lightest look that a turn
Of my shoulder and quickly, too quickly, I am gone?

By Disposition of Angels

MARIANNE MOORE

Messengers much like ourselves? Explain it.
Steadfastness the darkness makes explicit?
Something heard most clearly when not near it?
    Above particularities,
these unparticularities praise cannot violate.
    One has seen, in such steadiness never deflected,
    how by darkness a star is perfected.

Star that does not ask me if I see it?
Fir that would not wish me to uproot it?
Speech that does not ask me if I hear it?
    Mysteries expound mysteries.
Steadier than steady, star dazzling me, live and elate,
    no need to say, how like some we have known; too like her,
    too like him, and a-quiver forever.

PART TWO

Talking with Angels

What is it like to come close to an angel, or to listen to angelic tappings and whisperings, advice and prophecy? The stories and poems in this section present a spectrum of angels who come down to earth, or who meet people halfway. Angels can become astonishingly human companions, just as humans—in their mystery and their splendid otherness—can become astonishingly angel-like. Intervening in human lives, such angels have the power to help people change their life-stories. The angels offer knowledge, of God and of human history, that people do well to heed, for an angel, in these writings, is an utterly reliable narrator. This truthfulness is what makes such angels extraordinary, and not only welcome, but necessary.

After Midnight, the Fifth Month

JACQUELINE OSCHEROW

I am becoming a cathedral! My
Belly rises from the bed like a tiny
Model of the Florence *Cupolone*.
Probably a belly just like this
Inspired Brunelleschi's great design:
The original, the perfect, home.
There is a tapping from the inside,
Gentle, almost imperceptible,
Like piano hammers touching piano strings.
And I am fluent in these first attempts
At language; I am turned to someone else.
There *is* life beyond our own. Gabriel
Whispers, softly fluttering his wings,
With every touch a hushed annunciation.

The Wish

EINAR KVARAN

Translated by Jacob Wittmer Hartmann

· I ·

This must be a remarkable story for it took place both in heaven and on earth. It is about a tiny little squirt of an angel. His name was Jonas and he lived in heaven. He was in dreadful trouble. The story does not state precisely what he had done, but it must have been some unheard-of blunder he had made. He had by some foolishness thrown everything into commotion in heaven, where all is supposed to be perfect peace and calm.

Gabriel, the archangel, took up the matter gravely. He was completely dumbfounded by Jonas's conduct—that he, an angel in heaven, should behave like a fool!

"You will have to go down to the abode of men and stay there for some time," said Gabriel; for the abode of men is the reformatory of heaven.

Jonas thought it exasperating to be sentenced to the reformatory after having been an angel in heaven. To him it seemed reasonable that a station of such dignity should be taken into account, but he did not talk back; the powers of heaven are imposing and he knew there was not much to be gained by disputing the judge. So he remained silent and covered his face with his hands.

"You will have sore trials there," said Gabriel.

"How shall I go about this?" asked Jonas.

He began to have his doubts. He was not familiar with any place except heaven.

"We'll take care of that. We won't let this get the better of us. We've never had any difficulty in that respect." The archangel laughed at Jonas who couldn't imagine any way of getting into a scrape on earth.

Jonas bowed his head again and covered his face with his hands.

"The dangers of death will surround you. The vast rivers of perdition will terrify you. The snares of destruction will enclose you, as they enclosed our friend King David," said Gabriel.

"Good Lord!" said the little squirt of an angel in a low voice.

"Such things are nothing but daily occurrences on earth. Nobody pays any attention to them except those to whom these things happen," said Gabriel.

Jonas shook like a leaf in the wind. Terror gripped his heart with iron clutches, but he still sat with his head bowed down and his face covered with his hands.

"Down on earth moreover," said the archangel, "there are countless souls who think that they can't do any good deeds, although there are also others who perform nothing but good deeds all day long. Now one of them will have an opportunity to do an act of charity for you. That will strengthen him, and when the act of charity is accomplished you can come back here."

At that Jonas looked up. "How can I reward the act of charity?" he asked.

"The act of charity will reward itself," replied the archangel.

But now Jonas had become determined. "You must see yourself, powerful archangel, that although this has happened to me, I am nevertheless a heavenly angel, and cannot go about on earth and accept big favors from men without giving them something in return. That would be a disgrace for me and for heaven too."

He urged this with such obstinacy and eagerness that the archangel finally yielded to him.

"You may then grant one wish."

"Good! Thank you, Sir Archangel."

"I hope that nothing foolish will be asked but I am afraid it will be. Men are rather lacking in good sense. Try to see to it that we won't have to grant just any absurdity. Well, good-bye."

Jonas disappeared from heaven.

· II ·

"This is terrible weather," said old Sigurbjorg drawing her triangular shawl closer around the front of her neck and jerking her shoulders up to her ears as though suffering from a chill. "This is just like—" She checked herself and was silent. She did not want to mention the day that had almost escaped her lips. She knew that Thorunn could not stand it and would begin to weep.

"Yes, may God help all those who are out now whether on sea or land," said Thorunn, passing her hand over her pretty, young and freckled face. "That's the way it was when he—" she broke off and began to weep.

The weather was awful. The snowstorm beat against the rickety cottage and shook it like a rag. The snow was filling the window recess and though it was only noon it was already getting dark inside. When at last the sky cleared and faint glimpses could be seen of the coal-black rocky mountain ridges, their features seemed viciously distorted in the blanket of snow which surrounded them. The violent storm howled around them as if the irascible and malevolent powers of the universe were laughing a sardonic laugh at men.

It seemed lonely there in the hut for the two who were all by themselves. It had been so ever since Thorsteinn had left for the fishing village to hire himself out as a fisherman, but many times more lonely since the time when they knew that he had drowned.

"All the worse that he should leave her in such a terrible situation and without even so much consideration as to marry her," said old Sigurbjorg often to herself, but she never said it aloud. Not for anything would she have saddened Thorunn, not by a single word.

They sat opposite each other on their two beds. Thorunn was sewing a tiny little linen shirt, but it was getting too dark to see. Sigurbjorg was carding wool.

Thorunn was listening to the monotonous rasping of the woolcombs and was trying to find in it some tune for her amusement, but she did not succeed. There was more music in the raging snowstorm but its tunes were so terrible.

"I think I better begin spinning that tuft of wool," said Sigurbjorg, laying aside the woolcombs.

"Can't you tell me a story? Somehow it seems so lonesome," said Thorunn.

Sigurbjorg thought for a moment. "I suppose you have heard about the apparition that Gudridur from Kambasel saw?"

"Oh, no, don't tell me anything about ghosts now."

Thorunn looked out through the window. The strong winds lightly touched the windowpanes that were not yet covered with snow, as they rushed by with fearful speed like ghosts that must hurry in order to get hold of somebody before he goes to bed.

"Can't you tell me some story that ends well—something about God fulfilling the wishes of men?"

"Hush! Quiet! God help us! What is that?"

Sigurbjorg listened. Thorunn also began to listen.

"It's nothing but the storm beating against the door of the house," said Thorunn.

"Quiet! Listen!"

Sigurbjorg held her breath.

"It's the door creaking, nothing else."

"The door doesn't wail."

"The wind wails. There isn't a sound in existence that can't be found in the wind. Sometimes it weeps."

"Yes, when your mind is on weeping."

"Sometimes it laughs."

"You have seldom heard it laugh in the last weeks."

"Sometimes it sings a cradle song. Sometimes it is angry and rebukes men. Then I get so frightened."

"Yes, I know you hear a good deal of nonsense," said Sigurbjorg. "But I've probably imagined hearing something this time!"

"Hush! Listen!" said Thorunn.

"Did you hear anything?"

"Yes, I heard something touch the door."

"It's the wind."

"Never mind—I'm going to the door."

Thorunn dashed along the hallway toward the entrance, and Sigurbjorg after her.

• III •

When they opened the door they were instantly covered with snow. The storm struck them full in the face and whirled far into the hall-way. A drift of snow was piled high against the door of the cottage and something was wailing in the drift.

"Who is there?" they both called.

Again they heard the wail, a moan of suffering, a cry of distress, but no distinct words. They rushed to the snowdrift again and there they found a man.

"Can't you stand up, my good man?" said Thorunn and began tugging at him.

"No, no!" whimpered the man.

They lifted him up between them, Thorunn by the shoulders and old Sigurbjorg by the feet, and they carried him in through the door with great difficulty.

"You can't do that, Thorunn. He's too heavy."

"Oh yes, I can. Let's go on."

But Thorunn had become exhausted.

"Let's change. I'll take him by the shoulders. Remember the condition you're in."

"No, no, I'm young and I'm stronger than you."

They went on through the hall with their burden, huffing and puffing and finally they succeeded in getting him into Thorunn's bed. They hurriedly took off his outer clothing which was wet with snow, and covered him up. Then they began to look him over. He seemed to them to have fainted for he was as pale as a corpse. His bright yellow hair was very curly. After a while he opened his eyes and smiled, but they thought he couldn't see them.

"How beautiful he is!" said old Sigurbjorg.

"Yes."

"And he's young. He's a child."

"Yes."

"He's like some kind of angel."

"Yes."

"Listen, Thorunn—I think he'll die."

"God help us! Why do you think so?"

"It seemed to me as if he were looking into heaven."

"We'll have to look and see whether he's injured—especially his feet," said Thorunn.

They took off his stockings and found that neither his feet nor his hands or face were frostbitten.

Thorunn sat down on the bed in front of him while Sigurbjorg stood by the bed, and both looked at him thoughtfully.

"Who can he be? He's not from this neighborhood. I wonder where he's going?" said Sigurbjorg.

They were silent for a while. Thorunn could not, of course, answer the questions.

"Do you know what I think?" said Thorunn.

"No."

"I don't think he's a native of this place."

"God be with us, for us to have a foreigner in the house now!"

"And my shawl torn like this! But do you think that this could be? Do you think any foreigner could have come up here into this remote valley in the middle of winter? What business might he have here?"

"I don't know."

"Do you suppose that he wants to do us any harm?"

"No, no, no! Besides, don't you see how sick he is?"

Thorunn was still watching the stranger, she had never taken her eyes off him. Sigurbjorg was watching Thorunn.

"You are becoming so strange, Thorunn. You're not getting ill, are you?"

"No."

"For God's sake, you mustn't go and get ill in this blizzard—and with this sick stranger in the house. What would I do alone here in this weather?"

In Sigurbjorg's voice there was both fear and a hint of persuasion as if it were entirely within Thorunn's power not to get ill in order to spare Sigurbjorg this trouble.

"There's nothing the matter with me."

"You seem to be in a trance. Why are you staring this way?"

"I see—"

"Well, what do you see?"

"I see something that looks like a halo around his head."

"Almighty God protect us! But you often see and hear such nonsense—suppose he were—"

"Suppose he were what?"

Sigurbjorg did not have so much power of imagination that she could get further in her conjectures, but she was so frightened that she hardly dared remain in the house, though she was compelled to stay. As frightening as the halo was which Thorunn had noticed, the snowstorm was even more frightening.

Thorunn did not leave the bed.

• IV •

Night had come. The window now had a white shutter because the window-recess was filled with snow. Sigurbjorg was snoring in her bed. A light was burning on a candle stump which was stuck in a wooden holder with a handle on it, which in turn was fastened in a hole in the panel of the bed and cast a faint glimmer through the room. Behind the head of the bed were dark shadows, and beyond the door there was pitch-black darkness.

Thorunn was aware of this darkness even when she was not thinking about it at all.

"God knows whether this candle will last out the night," she said to herself.

If it should burn out, she would have to go to another part of the cottage and find some other light. She was so short of candles that she could hardly afford to burn a light like this all night, and then—to go out into the dark all alone during the night! But she had not been able to go to sleep and to leave him there unconscious. One of them had to watch over him and Sigurbjorg had been so frightened.

She listened to the storm. She had often listened to it before, had often heard the tunes it sang, sometimes heavy and roaring, sometimes screaming and howling, but always terrible. Now she heard a word. She had never heard something like that before. Only one word! She heard the wind pass gently along the roof of the house and whisper: "Power! Power!"

She heard the wind raise its voice and say loudly: *"Power! Power!"*

And she heard the wind pass over the roof roaring like a bull: *"POWER! POW-ER!"*

Then the wind caught the house in its grip like an old woman of nasty temper snatches a little child, and it shook it back and forth until it trembled.

"I'm so sleepy. Or am I beginning to dream? Or has something come loose that is making all this rumpus and racket?"

The storm bellowed the same word, but louder than before.

"Yes, it has power enough! Everything which harms us has power enough! Oh, how tired I am!"

The tired feeling passed through Thorunn's body from head to toe. She was scarcely able to sit up.

Then the man opened his eyes and Thorunn felt that now he saw her. She did not notice the darkness anymore nor did she hear the raging storm, and she was no longer aware of her fatigue.

"These are heavenly eyes," she said to herself, and her soul drank their beauty like a refreshing draught.

"How are you feeling now?" she asked.

"I'll soon be quite well."

Was he predicting his death? Her soul was grave and fervent with compassion, but his voice resounded in her ears like a soft and gentle melody even though the man was silent.

"What is your name?" she asked.

"Jonas."

"Have you come from far away?"

"Far or near, that depends on how you look at it."

"Where do you live?"

"I don't want to tell you a lie, and if I were to tell you the truth, you wouldn't understand it and wouldn't believe it."

He watched her with his blue eyes full of heavenly mercy and peace and she looked at him with wondering joy.

"I believe it."

He looked at her very thoughtfully.

"Yes, I see you do. Tonight the devil of skepticism has left you. Tomorrow he'll return."

"I don't understand you."

"When we stop speaking you'll go to sleep. When you awake I'll have disappeared. Then you'll think that I've been nothing but a dream and a figment of your imagination. This has been the fate of all of us who have come here."

"Sigurbjorg saw you also."

The visitor smiled.

"She'll think that I was the devil."

"Where do you live? Tell me the truth! I'll believe."

"My home is in heaven."

She didn't think he was telling her a lie. She didn't think he was mentally deranged. She believed him. Such is the power of those who come from heaven while they tarry here below. She thought for a little while. Now she felt her tiredness again, like sharp pains, especially in her feet and head.

"Yes, it must be a long way from here," she said.

"What would you wish for yourself if you had one wish?"

"I don't know. I have not thought about it. I have never had any."

"Would you wish something for yourself or for somebody else?"

"For somebody else," she replied without stopping to think.

"Yes, I suspected that."

She felt that he was beginning to watch her again, and a warm stream of joy flowed anew through her body and soul. She had entirely forgotten her fatigue.

"Do you believe me?"

"Yes, I believe you."

"I give you one wish. What do you want?"

"I don't know."

But she believed and she began thinking about the worldly blessings that she had heard mentioned. She knew one man of wealth. He was unhappy from the cares of earning a living and ill health. Those who had power were slandered and defamed. Men of talent were sensitive, restless, and without peace. Those most likely to be contented were the stupidest.

"What do you wish?"

"I don't know."

Her tiredness returned. Her thoughts became confused and she was afraid that she might do something stupid.

"Such an hour of grace God will send me only once! I'll never have such an opportunity again and here I don't have enough wits about me to use it!" she said to herself.

"What wish do you have?"

"I don't know . . ."

The storm began to shake the house again. It still roared with the power which she lacked. Pains shot throughout her body, and the fatigue weighed heavily upon her like a pile of earth.

"I feel as if I could sleep, sleep, forever and ever."

"What do you wish?"

Then it was as if the tiredness and the roar of the storm kindled a light in her soul. The darkness of doubt vanished in a moment from her mind. All became a bright, shining certainty.

"What do you wish?"

"I wish that the child I'm carrying will find delight in every exertion."

The visitor became thoughtful.

"Your wish is granted," he said. "Now you'll go to sleep."

At the same moment Thorunn fell asleep leaning against the back of the bed.

• V •

Jonas had returned home.

"What was the wish?" asked Gabriel, the archangel.

Jonas told the whole story.

The matter began to look serious to Gabriel.

"The young woman has been rather greedy. Did you grant this?" he asked.

"Yes, of course," replied Jonas with greatest confidence. "You gave me permission, sir."

"But do you understand what is involved in this grant?"

"Yes, sir."

"No, I see that you don't understand. The young woman has overturned the destiny of heaven and earth. Her child will be uncontrollable and unconquerable. It'll simply smile at everything that is decreed for it to do. Its life on earth will become like life in heaven. It'll enjoy supreme bliss in the universe—that of finding inexhaustible power within itself. It'll become more than we, the archangels."

Then a voice could be heard, far, far down from the high vaults of the heavens, more powerful than the sound of a thousand streams, more gentle than little children's dreams. "But that is what they were all created for," said the voice.

And Gabriel and all the angels who stood around him bowed their heads in submissiveness and supplication.

A Dedication

 JAMES MERRILL

Hans, there are moments when the whole mind
Resolves into a pair of brimming eyes, or lips
Parting to drink from the deep spring of a death
That freshness they do not yet need to understand.
These are the moments, if ever, an angel steps
Into the mind, as kings into the dress
Of a poor goatherd, for their acts of charity.
There are moments when speech is but a mouth pressed
Lightly and humbly against the angel's hand.

It Had Wings

 ALLAN GURGANUS

For Bruce Saylor and Constance Beavon

Find a little yellow side street house. Put an older woman in it.
Dress her in that tatty favorite robe, pull her slippers up before the

sink, have her doing dishes, gazing nowhere—at her own backyard. Gazing everywhere. Something falls outside, loud. One damp thwunk into new grass. A meteor? She herself (retired from selling formal clothes at Wanamaker's, she herself—a widow and the mother of three scattered sons, she herself alone at home a lot these days) goes onto tiptoe, leans across a sinkful of suds, sees—out near her picnic table, something nude, white, overly-long. It keeps shivering. Both wings seem damaged.

"No way," she says. It appears human. Yes, it is a male one. It's face up and, you can tell, it is extremely male (uncircumcised). This old woman, pushing eighty, a history of aches, uses, fun—now presses one damp hand across her eyes. Blaming strain, the luster of new cataracts, she looks again. Still, it rests there on a bright air mattress of its own wings. Outer feathers are tough quills, broad at bottom as rowboat oars. The whole left wing bends far under. It looks hurt.

The widow, sighing, takes up her blue willow mug of heated milk. Shaking her head, muttering, she carries it out back. She moves so slow because: arthritis. It criticizes every step. It asks about the mug she holds, Do you really need this?

. . .

She stoops, creaky, beside what can only be a young angel, unconscious. Quick, she checks overhead, ready for what?—some TV news crew in a helicopter? She sees only a sky of the usual size, a Tuesday sky stretched between weekends. She allows herself to touch this thing's white forehead. She gets a mild electric shock. Then, odd, her tickled finger joints stop aching. They've hurt so long. A practical person, she quickly cures her other hand. The angel grunts but sounds pleased. His temperature's a hundred and fifty, easy—but for him, this seems somehow normal. "Poor thing," she says, and—careful—pulls his heavy curly head into her lap. The head hums like a phone knocked off its cradle. She scans for neighbors, hoping they'll come out, wishing they wouldn't, both.

"Look, will warm milk help?" She pours some down him. Her wrist brushes angel skin. Which pulls the way an ice tray begs whatever touches it. A thirty-year pain leaves her, enters him. Even her liver spots are lightening. He grunts with pleasure, soaking up all of it. Bold, she presses her worst hip deep into crackling feathers. The hip has been half numb since a silly fall last February. All stiffness leaves her. He goes, "Unhh." Her griefs seem to fatten him like vitamins. Bolder, she whispers private woes: the Medicare cuts, the sons too casual by half, the daughters-in-law not bad but not so great. These woes seem ended. "Nobody'll believe. Still, tell me some of it." She tilts nearer. Both his eyes stay shut but his voice, like clicks from a million crickets pooled, goes, "We're just another army. We all look alike—we didn't, before. It's not what you expect. We miss this other. Don't count on the next. Notice things here. We are just another army."

"Oh," she says.

Nodding, she feels limber now, sure as any girl of twenty. Admiring her unspeckled hands, she helps him rise. Wings serve as handles. Kneeling on damp ground, she watches him go staggering toward her barbecue pit. Awkward for an athlete, really awkward for an angel, the poor thing climbs up there, wobbly. Standing, he is handsome, but as a vase is handsome. When he turns this way, she sees his eyes. They're silver, each reflects her: a speck, pink, on green green grass.

She now fears he plans to take her up, as thanks. She presses both palms flat to dirt, says, "The house is finally paid off. —Not just yet," and smiles.

Suddenly he's infinitely infinitely more so. Silvery. Raw. Gleaming like a sunny monument, a clock. Each wing puffs, independent. Feathers sort and shuffle like three hundred packs of playing cards. Out flings either arm; knees dip low. Then up and off he shoves, one solemn grunt. Machete swipes cross her backyard, breezes cool her upturned face. Six feet overhead, he falters, whips in makeshift circles, manages to hold aloft, then go shrub-high, gutter-high. He avoids a messy tangle of phone lines now rocking from the wind of him. "Go, go," the widow, grinning, points the way. "Do. Yeah, good." He signals back at her, open-mouthed and left down here. First a glinting man-shaped kite, next an oblong of aluminum in sun. Now a new moon shrunk to decent star, one fleck, fleck's memory: usual Tuesday sky.

She kneels, panting, happier and frisky. She is hungry but must first rush over and tell Lydia next door. Then she pictures Lydia's worry lines bunching. Lydia will maybe phone the missing sons: "Come right home. Your Mom's inventing . . . company."

Maybe other angels have dropped into other Elm Street backyards? Behind fences, did neighbors help earlier hurt ones? Folks keep so much of the best stuff quiet, don't they.

Palms on knees, she stands, wirier. This retired saleswoman was the formal-gowns adviser to ten mayors' wives. She spent sixty years of nine-to-five on her feet. Scuffing indoors, now staring down at terry slippers, she decides, "Got to wash these next week."

Can a person who's just sighted her first angel already be mulling about laundry? Yes. The world is like that.

From her sink, she sees her own blue willow mug out there in the grass. It rests in muddy ruts where the falling body struck so hard. A neighbor's collie keeps barking. (It saw!) Okay. This happened. "So," she says.

And plunges hands into dishwater, still warm. Heat usually helps her achy joints feel agile. But fingers don't even hurt now. Her bad hip doesn't pinch one bit. And yet, sad, they all will. By suppertime, they will again remind her what usual suffering means. To her nimble underwater hands, the widow, staring straight ahead, announces, "I helped. He flew off stronger. I really egged him on. Like *any*body would've, really. Still, it was me. I'm not just somebody in a house. I'm not just somebody alone in a house. I'm not just somebody else alone in a house."

Feeling more herself, she finishes the breakfast dishes. In time for lunch. This old woman should be famous for all she has been through—today's angel, her years in sales, the sons and friends—she should be famous for her life. She knows things, she has seen so much. She's not famous.

Still, the lady keeps gazing past her kitchen café curtains, she keeps studying her own small tidy yard. An Anchor fence, the picnic table, a barbecue pit, new Bermuda grass. Hands braced on her sink's cool edge, she tips nearer a bright window.

She seems to be expecting something, expecting something decent. Her kitchen clock is ticking. That dog still barks to calm itself. And she keeps staring out: nowhere, everywhere. Spots on her hands are darkening again. And yet, she whispers, "I'm right here, ready. Ready for more."

Can you guess why this old woman's chin is lifted? Why does she breathe as if to show exactly how it's done? Why should both her shoulders, usually quite bent, brace so square just now?

She is guarding the world.
Only, nobody knows.

The Eating of the Little Scroll

 REVELATION 10

Then I saw another mighty angel coming down from heaven, wrapped in a cloud, with a rainbow over his head, and his face was like the sun, and his legs like pillars of fire. He had a little scroll open in his hand. And he set his right foot on the sea, and his left foot on the land, and called out with a loud voice, like a lion roaring; when he called out, the seven thunders sounded. And when the seven thunders had sounded, I was about to write, but I heard a voice from heaven saying, "Seal up what the seven thunders have said, and do not write it down." And the angel whom I saw standing on sea and land lifted up his right hand to heaven and swore by him who lives for ever and ever, who created heaven and what is in it, the earth and what is in it, and the sea and what is in it, that there should be no more delay, but that in the days of the trumpet call to be sounded by the seventh angel, the mystery of God, as he announced to his servants the prophets, should be fulfilled.

Then the voice which I had heard from heaven spoke to me

again, saying, "Go, take the scroll which is open in the hand of the angel who is standing on the sea and on the land." So I went to the angel and told him to give me the little scroll; and he said to me, "Take it and eat; it will be bitter to your stomach, but sweet as honey in your mouth." And I took the little scroll from the hand of the angel and ate it; it was sweet as honey in my mouth, but when I had eaten it my stomach was made bitter. And I was told, "You must again prophesy about many peoples and nations and tongues and kings."

Sarah's Laughter

 GENESIS 18:1–15

And the Lord appeared to him by the oaks of Mamre, as he sat at the door of his tent in the heat of the day. He lifted up his eyes and looked, and behold, three men stood in front of him. When he saw them, he ran from the tent door to meet them, and bowed himself to the earth, and said, "My lord, if I have found favor in your sight, do not pass by your servant. Let a little water be brought, and wash your feet, and rest yourselves under the tree, while I fetch a morsel of bread, that you may refresh yourselves, and after that you may pass on—since you have come to your servant." So they said, "Do as you have said." And Abraham hastened into the tent to Sarah, and said, "Make ready quickly three measures of fine meal, knead it, and make cakes." And Abraham ran to the herd, and took a calf, tender and good, and gave it to the servant, who hastened to prepare it. Then he took curds, and milk, and the calf which he had prepared, and set it before them; and he stood by them under the tree while they ate.

They said to him, "Where is Sarah your wife?" And he said, "She is in the tent." The Lord said, "I will surely return to you in the spring, and Sarah your wife shall have a son." And Sarah was listening at the tent door behind him. Now Abraham and Sarah were old, advanced in age; it had ceased to be with Sarah after the manner of women. So Sarah laughed to herself, saying, "After I have grown old, and my husband is old, shall I have pleasure?" The Lord said to Abraham, "Why did Sarah laugh, and say, 'Shall I indeed bear a child, now that I am old?' Is anything too hard for the Lord? At the appointed time I will return to you, in the spring, and Sarah shall have a son." But Sarah denied, saying, "I did not laugh"; for she was afraid. He said, "No, but you did laugh."

Isaac's Birth

 GENESIS 21:1–3

The Lord visited Sarah as he had said, and the Lord did to Sarah as he had promised. And Sarah conceived, and bore Abraham a son in his old age at the time of which God had spoken to him. Abraham called the name of his son who was born to him, whom Sarah bore him, Isaac.

Mother and Other: seeing through laughter

✍ PAMELA WHITE HADAS

I tag behind the servants who carry the plates
of dainties—excluding the ember-cakes of course—
then wait out of sight by the tent-flap to listen.
Would it be terrible to interrupt the conversation?
I do not usually eavesdrop, but in an emergency . . .
One of the strangers is predicting Abraham's son,
my son, and in a year from now. Sure thing. I am ninety.
Abraham . . . ? is ninety-nine.

> Ha!
> I laugh.
> I laugh behind the tent-flap—
> to myself, I hope—
> could they hear it?

I rush then into the quiet-as-death quiet
all at once eager to fill it up.

"We were about to ask after you, Sarah," states
one unintroduced as names are being mumbled by Abraham.
I look at their plates.
They are eating like birds, all of them.
And the one—called Michael, I think it is—
not enough even to fill
a goldfinch. I am afraid I seem nervous.
I suggest a smidgen of this or that—or are they full
already—maybe room for just some sesame

butter, grapes, dates . . . a sliver of melon? some honey?
Are the words coming out or not?
They are not eating enough even to make
decent scarecrows out of them. But all right. All right.
Maybe they were too busy talking. Maybe they are not
used to the food. Gabriel, just a little more?
I am not asking if they want any cake.
The silence—an enormous belly.

                          "What I came for"—
I turn to my husband—"is to say I'm sorry,
but the cakes are not fit for you to eat.
By that I mean"—I turn to the guests—"my husband is
allergic—not quite—but if you have no objection
to something made up by a woman in question,
I can wrap some up for you to take for later?"
"By all means, and thank you very much," says
the one called Michael. "But now have a cup of wine with us."
Abraham coughs. I blush.

                        And Raphael says, "Sarah, why
did you laugh just now?" "Laugh," I say,
"who laughed? The wind in that tree . . . ? Maybe Lilith . . ."
"But you *did* laugh," says Gabriel staring through me.
Michael looks at his plate and looks devious.
"All right, I heard you joking about us.
We are ninety and ninety-nine years old, after all,
old enough to beware of prophets that are false.
Is it a nice thing to do, to tease
an old man, and when he is being so generous?"

"You laughed."

"So? So I laughed. I admit it. I am the daughter
of a man, and the wife, but—now—to be the mother
of a multitude—it breaks me up—that's life."

I feel like a grenadilla bud about to burst.

"And I laughed because I already knew,
by a certain untimely curse that . . ." and I blush
again to think of the untouchable cakes.
Abraham chokes.
                    His strange guests get up to go.
I bleed for him.
                    It is too much, too much . . .
So I laugh.

From *Captain Stormfield's Visit to Heaven*
 MARK TWAIN

The very next instant a voice I knew sung out in a business kind
of a way—
   "A harp and a hymn-book, pair of wings and a halo, size 13, for
Cap'n Eli Stormfield, of San Francisco!—make him out a clean bill
of health, and let him in."

I opened my eyes. Sure enough, it was a Pi Ute Injun I used to know in Tulare County; mighty good fellow—I remembered being at his funeral, which consisted of him being burnt and the other Injuns gauming their faces with his ashes and howling like wild cats. He was powerful glad to see me, and you may make up your mind I was just as glad to see him, and felt that I was in the right kind of a heaven at last.

Just as far as your eye could reach, there was swarms of clerks, running and bustling around, tricking out thousands of Yanks and Mexicans and English and Arabs, and all sorts of people in their new outfits; and when they gave me my kit and I put on my halo and I took a look in the glass, I could have jumped over a house for joy, I was so happy. "Now *this* is something like!" says I. "Now," says I, "I'm all right—show me a cloud."

Inside of fifteen minutes I was a mile on my way towards the cloud-banks and about a million people along with me. Most of us tried to fly, but some got crippled and nobody made a success of it. So we concluded to walk, for the present, till we had had some wing practice.

We begun to meet swarms of folks who were coming back. Some had harps and nothing else; some had hymn-books and nothing else; some had nothing at all; all of them looked meek and uncomfortable; one young fellow hadn't anything left but his halo, and he was carrying that in his hand; all of a sudden he offered it to me and says—

"Will you hold it for me a minute?"

Then he disappeared in the crowd. I went on. A woman asked me to hold her palm branch, and then *she* disappeared. A girl got me to hold her harp for her, and by George, *she* disappeared; and so on and so on, till I was about loaded down to the guards. Then comes a smiling old gentleman and asked me to hold *his* things. I swabbed off the perspiration and says, pretty tart—

"I'll have to get you to excuse me, my friend,—*I* ain't no hatrack."

About this time I begun to run across piles of those traps, lying in the road. I just quietly dumped my extra cargo along with them. I looked around, and, Peters, that whole nation that was following me were loaded down the same as I'd been. The return crowd had got them to hold their things a minute, you see. They all dumped their loads, too, and we went on.

When I found myself perched on a cloud, with a million other people, I never felt so good in my life. Says I, "Now this is according to the promises; I've been having my doubts, but now I *am* in heaven, sure enough." I gave my palm branch a wave or two, for luck, and then I tautened up my harp-strings and struck in. Well, Peters, you can't imagine anything like the row we made. It was grand to listen to, and made a body thrill all over, but there was considerable many tunes going on at once, and that was a drawback to the harmony, you understand; and then there was a lot of Injun tribes, and they kept up such another war-whooping that they kind of took the tuck out of the music. By and by I quit performing, and judged I'd take a rest. There was quite a nice mild old gentleman sitting next me, and I noticed he didn't take a hand; I encouraged him, but he said he was naturally bashful, and was afraid to try before so many people. By and by the old gentleman said he never could seem to enjoy music somehow. The fact was, I was beginning to feel the same way; but I didn't say anything. Him and I had a considerable long silence, then, but of course it warn't noticeable in that place. After about sixteen or seventeen hours, during which I played and sung a little, now and then—always the same tune, because I didn't know any other—I laid down my harp and begun to fan myself with my palm branch. Then we both got to sighing pretty regular. Finally, says he—

"Don't you know any tune but the one you've been pegging at all day?"

"Not another blessed one," says I.

"Don't you reckon you could learn another one?" says he.

"Never," says I; "I've tried to, but I couldn't manage it."

"It's a long time to hang to the one—eternity, you know."

"Don't break my heart," says I; "I'm getting low-spirited enough already."

After another long silence, says he—

"Are you glad to be here?"

Says I, "Old man, I'll be frank with you. This *ain't* just as near my idea of bliss as I thought it was going to be, when I used to go to church."

Says he, "What do you say to knocking off and calling it half a day?"

"That's me," says I. "I never wanted to get off watch so bad in my life."

So we started. Millions were coming to the cloud-bank all the time, happy and hosannahing; millions were leaving it all the time, looking mighty quiet, I tell you. We laid for the newcomers, and pretty soon I'd got them to hold all my things a minute, and then I was a free man again and most outrageously happy. Just then I ran across old Sam Bartlett, who had been dead a long time, and stopped to have a talk with him. Says I—

"Now tell me—is this to go on forever? Ain't there anything else for a change?"

Says he—

"I'll set you right on that point very quick. People take the figurative language of the Bible and the allegories for literal, and the first thing they ask for when they get here is a halo and a harp, and so on. Nothing that's harmless and reasonable is refused a body here, if he asks it in the right spirit. So they are outfitted with these things without a word. They go and sing and play just about one day, and that's the last you'll ever see them in the choir. They don't need anybody to tell them that that sort of thing wouldn't make a heaven—at least not a heaven that a sane man could stand a week and remain sane. That cloud-bank is placed where the noise can't disturb the old inhabitants, and so there ain't any harm in letting everybody get up there and cure himself as soon as he comes.

"Now you just remember this—heaven is as blissful and lovely as it can be; but it's just the busiest place you ever heard of. There ain't any idle people here after the first day. Singing hymns and waving palm branches through all eternity is pretty when you hear about it in the pulpit, but it's as poor a way to put in valuable time as a body could contrive. It would just make a heaven of warbling ignoramuses, don't you see? Eternal Rest sounds comforting in the pulpit, too. Well, you try it once, and see how heavy time will hang on your hands. Why, Stormfield, a man like you, that had been active and stirring all his life, would go mad in six months in a heaven where he hadn't anything to do. Heaven is the very last place to come to *rest* in—and don't you be afraid to bet on that!"

Says I—

"Sam, I'm as glad to hear it as I thought I'd be sorry. I'm glad I come, now."

Says he—

"Cap'n, ain't you pretty physically tired?"

Says I—

"Sam, it ain't my name for it! I'm dog-tired."

"Just so—just so. You've earned a good sleep, and you'll get it. You've earned a good appetite, and you'll enjoy your dinner. It's the same here as it is on earth—you've got to earn a thing, square and honest, before you enjoy it. You can't enjoy first and earn afterwards. But there's this difference, here: you can choose your own occupation, and all the powers of heaven will be put forth to help you make a success of it, if you do your level best. The shoemaker on earth that had the soul of a poet in him won't have to make shoes here."

"Now that's all reasonable and right," says I. "Plenty of work, and the kind you hanker after; no more pain, no more suffering—"

"Oh, hold on; there's plenty of pain here—but it don't kill. There's plenty of suffering here, but it don't last. You see, happiness ain't a *thing in itself*—it's only a *contrast* with something that ain't pleasant. That's all it is. There ain't a thing you can mention that is happiness in its own self—it's only so by contrast with the other thing. And so, as soon as the novelty is over and the force of the contrast dulled, it ain't happiness any longer, and you have to get something fresh. Well, there's plenty of pain and suffering in heaven—consequently there's plenty of contrasts, and just no end of happiness."

Says I, "It's the sensiblest heaven I've heard of, yet, Sam, though it's about as different from the one I was brought up on as a live princess is different from her own wax figger."

Along in the first months I knocked around about the Kingdom, making friends and looking at the country, and finally settled down in a pretty likely region, to have a rest before taking another start. I went on making acquaintances and gathering up information. I had a good deal of talk with an old bald-headed angel by the name of Sandy McWilliams. He was from somewhere in New Jersey. I went about with him, considerable. We used to lay around, warm afternoons, in the shade of a rock, on some meadow-ground that was pretty high and out of the marshy slush of his cranberry-farm, and there we used to talk about all kinds of things, and smoke pipes. One day, says I—

"About how old might you be, Sandy?"

"Seventy-two."

"I judged so. How long you been in heaven?"

"Twenty-seven years, come Christmas."

"How old was you when you come up?"

"Why, seventy-two, of course."

"You can't mean it!"

"Why can't I mean it?"

"Because, if you was seventy-two then, you are naturally ninety-nine now."

"No, but I ain't. I stay the same age I was when I come."

"Well," says I, "come to think, there's something just here that I want to ask about. Down below, I always had an idea that in heaven we would all be young, and bright, and spry."

"Well, you *can* be young if you want to. You've only got to wish."

"Well, then, why didn't you wish?"

"I did. They all do. You'll try it, some day, like enough; but you'll get tired of the change pretty soon."

"Why?"

"Well, I'll tell you. Now you've always been a sailor; did you ever try some other business?"

"Yes, I tried keeping grocery, once, up in the mines; but I couldn't stand it; it was too dull—no stir, no storm, no life about it; it was like being part dead and part alive, both at the same time. I wanted to be one thing or t'other. I shut up shop pretty quick and went to sea."

"That's it. Grocery people like it, but you couldn't. You see you wasn't used to it. Well, I wasn't used to being young, and I couldn't seem to take any interest in it. I was strong, and handsome, and had curly hair,—yes, and wings, too!—gay wings like a butterfly. I went to picnics and dances and parties with the fellows, and tried to carry on and talk nonsense with the girls, but it wasn't any use; I couldn't take to it—fact is, it was an awful bore. What I wanted was early to bed and early to rise, and something to *do*; and when my work was done, I wanted to sit quiet, and smoke and think—not tear around with a parcel of giddy young kids. You can't think what I suffered whilst I was young."

"How long was you young?"

"Only two weeks. That was plenty for me. Laws, I was so lonesome! You see, I was full of the knowledge and experience of seventy-two years; the deepest subject those young folks could strike was only *a-b-c* to me. And to hear them argue—oh, my! it would have been funny, if it hadn't been so pitiful. Well, I was so hungry for the ways and the sober talk I was used to, that I tried to ring in with the old people, but they wouldn't have it. They considered me a conceited young up-start, and gave me the cold shoulder. Two weeks was a-plenty for me. I was glad to get back my bald head again, and my pipe, and my old drowsy reflections in the shade of a rock or a tree."

"Well," says I, "do you mean to say you're going to stand still at seventy-two, forever?"

"I don't know, and I ain't particular. But I ain't going to drop back to twenty-five any more—I know that, mighty well. I know a sight more than I did twenty-seven years ago, and I enjoy learning, all the time, but I don't seem to get any older. That is, bodily—my mind gets older, and stronger, and better seasoned, and more satisfactory."

Says I, "If a man comes here at ninety, don't he ever set himself back?"

"Of course he does. He sets himself back to fourteen; tries it a couple of hours, and feels like a fool; sets himself forward to twenty; it ain't much improvement; tries thirty, fifty, eighty, and finally ninety—finds he is more at home and comfortable at the same old figure he is used to than any other way. Or, if his mind begun to fail him on earth at eighty, that's where he finally sticks up here. He sticks at the place where his mind was last at its best, for there's where his enjoyment is best, and his ways most set and established."

"Does a chap of twenty-five stay always twenty-five, and look it?"

"If he is a fool, yes. But if he is bright, and ambitious and industrious, the knowledge he gains and the experience he has, change his ways and thoughts and likings, and make him find his best pleasure in the company of people above that age; so he allows his body to take on that look of as many added years as he needs to make him comfortable and proper in that sort of society; he lets his body go on taking the look of age, according as he progresses, and by and by he will be bald and wrinkled outside, and wise and deep within."

"Babies the same?"

"Babies the same. Laws, what asses we used to be, on earth, about these things! We said we'd be always young in heaven. We didn't say *how* young—we didn't think of that, perhaps—that is, we didn't all think alike, anyway. When I was a boy of seven, I suppose I thought we'd all be twelve, in heaven; when I was twelve, I suppose I thought we'd all be eighteen or twenty in heaven; when I was forty, I begun to go back; I remember I hoped we'd all be about *thirty* years old in heaven. Neither a man nor a boy ever thinks the age he *has* is exactly the best one—he puts the *right* age a few years older or a few years younger than he is. Then he makes the ideal age the general age of the heavenly people. And he expects everybody to *stick* at that age—stand stock-still—and expects them to enjoy it!— Now just think of the idea of standing still in heaven! Think of a heaven made up entirely of hoop-rolling, marble-playing cubs of seven years!—or of awkward, diffident, sentimental immaturities of nineteen!—or of vigorous people of thirty, healthy-minded, brimming with ambition, but chained hand and foot to that one age and its limitations like so many helpless galley-slaves! Think of the dull sameness of a society made up of people all of one age and one set of looks, habits, tastes and feelings. Think how superior to it earth would be, with its variety of types and faces and ages, and the enlivening attrition of the myriad interests that come into pleasant collision in such a variegated society."

"Look here," says I, "do you know what you're doing?"

"Well, what am I doing?"

"You are making heaven pretty comfortable in one way, but you are playing the mischief with it in another."

"How d'you mean?"

"Well," I says, "take a young mother that's lost her child, and—"

"Sh!" he says. "Look!"

It was a woman. Middle-aged, and had grizzled hair. She was walking slow, and her head was bent down, and her wings hanging limp and droopy; and she looked ever so tired, and was crying, poor thing! She passed along by, with her head down, that way, and the tears running down her face, and didn't see us. Then Sandy said, low and gentle, and full of pity:

"*She's* hunting for her child! No, *found* it, I reckon. Lord, how she's changed! But I recognized her in a minute, though it's twenty-seven years since I saw her. A young mother she was, about twenty-two or four, or along there; and blooming and lovely and sweet—oh, just a flower! And all her heart and all her soul was wrapped up in her child, her little girl, two years old. And it died, and she went wild with grief, just wild! Well, the only comfort she had was that she'd see her child again, in heaven—'never more to part,' she said, and kept on saying it over and over, 'never more to part.' And the words made her happy; yes, they did; they made her joyful; and when I was dying, twenty-seven years ago, she told me to find her child the first thing, and say she was coming—'soon, soon, *very* soon, she hoped and believed!' "

"Why, it's pitiful, Sandy."

He didn't say anything for a while, but sat looking at the ground, thinking. Then he says, kind of mournful:

"And now she's come!"

"Well? Go on."

"Stormfield, maybe she hasn't found the child, but *I* think she has. Looks so to me. I've seen cases before. You see, she's kept that child in her head just the same as it was when she jounced it in her arms a little chubby thing. But here it didn't elect to *stay* a child. No, it elected to grow up, which it did. And in these twenty-seven years it has learned all the deep scientific learning there is to learn, and is studying and studying and learning and learning more and more, all the time, and don't give a damn for anything *but* learning; just learning, and discussing gigantic problems with people like herself."

"Well?"

"Stormfield, don't you see? Her mother knows *cranberries*, and how to tend them, and pick them, and put them up, and market them; and not another blamed thing! Her and her daughter can't be any more company for each other *now* than mud turtle and bird o' paradise. Poor thing, she was looking for a baby to jounce; *I* think she's struck a disappointment."

"Sandy, what will they do—stay unhappy forever in heaven?"

"No, they'll come together and get adjusted by and by. But not this year, and not next. By and by."

The Angel of the Bridge

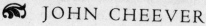 JOHN CHEEVER

You may have seen my mother waltzing on ice skates in Rockefeller Center. She's seventy-eight years old now but very wiry, and she wears a red velvet costume with a short skirt. Her tights are flesh-colored, and she wears spectacles and a red ribbon in her white hair, and she waltzes with one of the rink attendants. I don't know why I should find the fact that she waltzes on ice skates so disconcerting, but I do. I avoid that neighborhood whenever I can during the winter months, and I never lunch in the restaurants on the rink. Once when I was passing that way, a total stranger took me by the arm and, pointing to Mother, said, "Look at that crazy old dame." I was very embarrassed. I suppose I should be grateful for the fact that she amuses herself and is not a burden to me, but I sincerely wish she had hit on some less conspicuous recreation. Whenever I see gracious old ladies arranging chrysanthemums and pouring tea, I think of my own mother, dressed like a hat-check girl, pushing some paid rink attendant around the ice, in the middle of the third-biggest city of the world.

My mother learned to figure-skate in the little New England village of St. Botolphs, where we come from, and her waltzing is an expression of her attachment to the past. The older she grows, the more she longs for the vanishing and provincial world of her youth. She is a hardy woman, as you can imagine, but she does not relish change. I arranged one summer for her to fly to Toledo and visit friends. I drove her to the Newark airport. She seemed troubled by the airport waiting room, with its illuminated advertisements, vaulted ceiling, and touching and painful scenes of separation played out to an uproar of continuous tango music. She did not seem to find it in any way interesting or beautiful, and compared to the railroad station in St. Botolphs it was indeed a strange background against which to take one's departure. The flight was delayed for an hour, and we sat in the waiting room. Mother looked tired and old. When we had been waiting half an hour, she began to have some noticeable difficulty in breathing. She spread a hand over the front of her dress and began to gasp deeply, as if she was in pain. Her face got mottled and red. I pretended not to notice this. When the plane was announced, she got to her feet and exclaimed, "I want to go home! If I have to die suddenly, I don't want to die in a flying machine." I cashed in her ticket and drove her back to her apartment, and I have never mentioned this seizure to her or to anyone, but her capricious, or perhaps neurotic, fear of dying in a plane crash was the first insight I had into how, as she grew older, her way was strewn with invisible rocks and lions and how eccentric were the paths she took, as the world seemed to change its boundaries and become less and less comprehensible.

At the time of which I'm writing, I flew a great deal myself. My business was in Rome, New York, San Francisco, and Los Angeles, and I sometimes traveled as often as once a month between these cities. I liked the flying. I liked the incandescence of the sky at high altitudes. I liked all eastward flights where you can see from the ports the edge of night move over the continent and where, when it is four o'clock by your California watch, the housewives of Garden City are washing up the supper dishes and the stewardess in the plane is passing a second round of drinks. Toward the end of the flight, the air is stale. You are tired. The gold thread in the upholstery scratches your cheek, and there is a momentary feeling of forlornness, a sulky and childish sense of estrangement. You find good companions, of course, and bores, but most of the errands we run at such high altitudes are humble and terrestrial. That old lady, flying over the North Pole, is taking a jar of calf's-foot jelly to her sister in Paris, and the man beside her sells imitation-leather inner soles. Flying westward one dark night—we had crossed the Continental Divide, but we were still an hour out of Los Angeles and had not begun our descent, and were at such an altitude that the sense of houses, cities, and people below us was lost—I saw a formation, a trace of light, like the lights that burn along a shore. There was no shore in that part of the world, and I knew I would never know if the edge of the desert or some bluff or mountain accounted for this hoop of light, but it seemed, in its obscurity—and at that velocity and height—like the emergence of a new world, a gentle hint at my own obsolescence, the lateness of my time of life, and my inability to understand the things I often see. It was a pleasant feeling, completely free of regret, of being caught in some observable midpassage, the farther reaches of which might be understood by my sons.

I liked to fly, as I say, and had none of my mother's anxieties. It was my older brother—her darling—who was to inherit her resoluteness, her stubbornness, her table silver, and some of her eccentricities. One evening, my brother—I had not seen him for a year or so—called and asked if he could come for dinner. I was happy to invite him. We live on the eleventh floor of an apartment house, and at seven-thirty he telephoned from the lobby and asked me to come down. I thought he must have something to tell me privately, but when we met in the lobby he got into the automatic elevator with me and we started up. As soon as the doors closed, he showed the same symptoms of fear I had seen in my mother. Sweat stood out on his forehead, and he gasped like a runner.

"What in the world is the matter?" I asked.

"I'm afraid of elevators," he said miserably.

"But what are you afraid of?"

"I'm afraid the building will fall down."

I laughed—cruelly, I guess. For it all seemed terribly funny, his vision of the buildings of New York banging against one another like ninepins as they fell to the earth. There has always been a strain of jealousy in our feelings about one another, and I am aware, at some obscure level, that he makes more money and has more of everything than I, and to see him humiliated—crushed—saddened me but at the same time and in spite of myself made me feel that I had taken a stunning lead in the race for honors that is at the bottom of our relationship. He is the oldest, he is the favorite, but watching his misery in the elevator I felt that he was merely my poor old brother, overtaken by his worries. He stopped in the hallway to recover his composure, and explained that he had been suffering from this phobia for over a year. He was going to a psychiatrist, he said. I couldn't see that it had done him any good. He was all right once he got out of the elevator, but I noticed that he stayed away from the windows. When it was time to go, I walked him out to the corridor. I was curious. When the elevator reached our floor, he turned to me and said, "I'm afraid I'll have to take the stairs." I led him to the stairway, and we climbed slowly down the eleven flights. He clung to the railing. We said goodbye in the lobby; and I went up in the elevator, and told my wife about his fear that the building might fall down. It seemed strange and sad to her, and it did to me, too, but it also seemed terribly funny.

It wasn't terribly funny when, a month later, the firm he worked for moved to the fifty-second floor of a new office building and he had to resign. I don't know what reasons he gave. It was another six months before he could find a job in a third-floor office. I once saw him on a winter dusk at the corner of Madison Avenue and Fifty-ninth Street, waiting for the light to change. He appeared to be an intelligent, civilized, and well-dressed man, and I wondered how many of the men waiting with him to cross the street made their way as he did through a ruin of absurd delusions, in which the street might appear to be a torrent and the approaching cab driven by the angel of death.

He was quite all right on the ground. My wife and I went to his house in New Jersey, with the children, for a weekend, and he looked healthy and well. I didn't ask about his phobia. We drove back to New York on Sunday afternoon. As we approached the George Washington Bridge, I saw a thunderstorm over the city. A strong wind struck the car the moment we were on the bridge, and nearly took the wheel out of my hand. It seemed to me that I could feel the huge structure swing. Halfway across the bridge, I thought I felt the roadway begin to give. I could see no signs of a collapse, and yet I was convinced that in another minute the bridge would split in two and hurl the long lines of Sunday traffic into the dark water below us. This imagined disaster was terrifying. My legs got so weak that I was not sure I could brake the car if I needed to. Then it became difficult for me to breathe. Only by opening my mouth and gasping did I seem able to take in any air. My blood pressure was affected and I began to feel a darkening of my vision. Fear has always seemed to me to run a course, and at its climax the body and perhaps the spirit defend themselves by drawing on some new and fresh source of strength. Once over the center of the bridge, my pain and terror began to diminish. My wife and the children were admiring the storm, and they did not seem to have noticed my spasm. I was afraid both that the bridge would fall down and that they might observe my panic.

I thought back over the weekend for some incident that might account for my preposterous fear that the George Washington Bridge would blow away in a thunderstorm, but it had been a pleasant weekend, and even under the most exaggerated scrutiny I couldn't uncover any source of morbid nervousness or anxiety. Later in the week, I had to drive to Albany, and, although the day was clear and windless, the memory of my first attack was too keen; I hugged the east bank of the river as far north as Troy, where I found a small, old-fashioned bridge that I could cross comfortably. This meant going fifteen or twenty miles out of my way, and it is humiliating to have your travels obstructed by barriers that are senseless and invisible. I drove back from Albany by the same route, and next morning I went to the family doctor and told him I was afraid of bridges.

He laughed. "You, of all people," he said scornfully. "You'd better take hold of yourself."

"But Mother is afraid of airplanes," I said. "And Brother hates elevators."

"Your mother is past seventy," he said, "and one of the most remarkable women I've ever known. I wouldn't bring *her* into this. What *you* need is a little more backbone."

This was all he had to say, and I asked him to recommend an analyst. He does not include psychoanalysis in medical science, and told me I would be wasting my time and money, but, yielding to his obligation to be helpful, he gave me the name and address of a psychiatrist, who told me that my fear of bridges was the surface manifestation of a deep-seated anxiety and that I would have to have a full analysis. I didn't have the time, or the money, or above all, the confidence in the doctor's methods to put myself in his hands, and I said I would try and muddle through.

There are obviously areas of true and false pain, and my pain was meretricious, but how could I convince my lights and vitals of this? My youth and childhood had their deeply troubled and their jubilant years, and could some repercussions from this past account for my fear of heights? The thought of a life determined by hidden obstacles was unacceptable, and I decided to take the advice of the family doctor and ask more of myself. I had to go to Idlewild later in the week, and, rather than take a bus or a taxi, I drove the car myself. I nearly lost consciousness on the Triborough Bridge. When I got to the airport I ordered a cup of coffee, but my hand was shaking so I spilled the coffee on the counter. The man beside me was amused and said that I must have put in quite a night. How could I tell him that I had gone to bed early and sober but that I was afraid of bridges?

I flew to Los Angeles late that afternoon. It was one o'clock by my watch when we landed. It was only ten o'clock in California. I was tired and took a taxi to the hotel where I always stay, but I couldn't sleep. Outside my hotel window was a monumental statue of a young woman, advertising a Las Vegas night club. She revolves slowly in a beam of light. At 2 A.M. the light is extinguished, but she goes on restlessly turning all through the night. I have never seen her cease her turning, and I wondered, that night, when they greased her axle and washed her shoulders. I felt some affection for her, since neither of us could rest, and I wondered if she had a family—a stage mother, perhaps, and a compromised and broken-spirited father who drove a municipal bus on the West Pico line? There was a restaurant across the street, and I watched a drunken woman in a sable cape being led out to a car. She twice nearly fell. The crosslights from the open door, the lateness, her drunken-ness, and the solicitude of the man with her made the scene, I thought, worried and lonely. Then two cars that seemed to be rac-ing down Sunset Boulevard pulled up at a traffic light under my window. Three men piled out of each car and began to slug one an-other. You could hear the blows land on bone and cartilage. When the light changed, they got back into their cars and raced off. The fight, like the hoop of light I had seen from the plane, seemed like the signs of a new world, but in this case an emergence of brutality and chaos. Then I remembered that I was to go to San Francisco on Thursday, and was expected in Berkeley for lunch. This meant crossing the San Francisco–Oakland Bay Bridge, and I reminded myself to take a cab both ways and leave the car I rented in San Francisco in the hotel garage. I tried again to reason out my fear that the bridge would fall. Was I the victim of some sexual disloca-tion? My life has been promiscuous, carefree, and a source of im-mense pleasure, but was there some secret here that would have to be mined by a professional? Were all my pleasures impostures and evasions, and was I really in love with my old mother in her skating costume?

Looking at Sunset Boulevard at three in the morning, I felt that my terror of bridges was an expression of my clumsily concealed horror of what is becoming of the world. I can drive with composure through the outskirts of Cleveland and Toledo—past the birthplace of the Polish Hot Dog, the Buffalo Burger stands, the used-car lots, and the architectural monotony. I claim to enjoy walking down Hollywood Boulevard on a Sunday afternoon. I have cheerfully praised the evening sky hanging beyond the disheveled and expatriated palm trees on Doheny Boulevard, stuck up against the incandescence, like rank upon rank of wet mops. Duluth and East Seneca are charming, and if they aren't, just look away. The hideousness of the road between San Francisco and Palo Alto is nothing more than the search of honest men and women for a decent place to live. The same thing goes for San Pedro and all that coast. But the height of bridges seemed to be one link I could not forge or fasten in this hypocritical chain of acceptances. The truth is, I hate freeways and Buffalo Burgers. Expatriated palm trees and monotonous housing developments depress me. The continuous music on special-fare trains exacerbates my feelings. I detest the destruction of familiar landmarks, I am deeply troubled by the misery and drunkenness I find among my friends, I abhor the dishonest practices I see. And it was at the highest point in the arc of a bridge that I became aware suddenly of the depth and bitterness of my feelings about modern life, and of the profoundness of my yearning for a more vivid, simple, and peaceable world.

But I couldn't reform Sunset Boulevard, and until I could, I couldn't drive across the San Francisco–Oakland Bay Bridge. What *could* I do? Go back to St. Botolphs, wear a Norfolk jacket, and play cribbage in the firehouse? There was only one bridge in the village, and you could throw a stone across the river there.

.   .   .

I got home from San Francisco on Saturday, and found my daughter back from school for the weekend. On Sunday morning, she asked me to drive her to the convent school in Jersey where she is a student. She had to be back in time for nine-o'clock Mass, and we left our apartment in the city a little after seven. We were talking and laughing, and I had approached and was in fact on the George Washington Bridge without having remembered my weakness. There were no preliminaries this time. The seizure came with a rush. The strength went out of my legs, I gasped for breath, and felt the terrifying loss of sight. I was, at the same time, determined to conceal these symptoms from my daughter. I made the other side of the bridge, but I was violently shaken. My daughter didn't seem to have noticed. I got her to school in time, kissed her goodbye, and started home. There was no question of my crossing the George Washington Bridge again, and I decided to drive north to Nyack and cross on the Tappan Zee Bridge. It seemed, in my memory, more gradual and more securely anchored to its shores. Driving up the parkway on the west shore, I decided that oxygen was what I needed, and I opened all the windows of the car. The fresh air seemed to help, but only momentarily. I could feel my sense of reality ebbing. The roadside and the car itself seemed to have less substance than a dream. I had some friends in the neighborhood, and

I thought of stopping and asking them for a drink, but it was only a little after nine in the morning, and I could not face the embarrassment of asking for a drink so early in the day, and of explaining that I was afraid of bridges. I thought I might feel better if I talked to someone, and I stopped at a gas station and bought some gas, but the attendant was laconic and sleepy, and I couldn't explain to him that his conversation might make the difference between life and death. I had got onto the Thruway by then, and I wondered what alternatives I had if I couldn't cross the bridge. I could call my wife and ask her to make some arrangements for removing me, but our relationship involves so much self-esteem and face that to admit openly to this foolishness might damage our married happiness. I could call the garage we use and ask them to send up a man to chauffeur me home. I could park the car and wait until one o'clock, when the bars opened, and fill up on whiskey, but I had spent the last of my money for gasoline. I decided to take a chance, and turned onto the approach to the bridge.

All the symptoms returned, and this time they were much worse than ever. The wind was knocked out of my lungs as by a blow. My equilibrium was so shaken that the car swerved from one lane into another. I drove to the side and pulled on the hand brake. The loneliness of my predicament was harrowing. If I had been miserable with romantic love, racked with sickness, or beastly drunk, it would have seemed more dignified. I remembered my brother's face, sallow and greasy with sweat in the elevator, and my mother in her red skirt, one leg held gracefully aloft as she coasted backward in the arms of a rink attendant, and it seemed to me that we were all three characters in some bitter and sordid tragedy, carrying impossible burdens and separated from the rest of mankind by our misfortunes. My life was over, and it would never come back, everything that I loved—blue-sky courage, lustiness, the natural grasp of things. It would never come back. I would end up in the psychiatric ward of the county hospital, screaming that the bridges, all the bridges in the world, were falling down.

Then a young girl opened the door of the car and got in. "I didn't think anyone would pick me up on the bridge," she said. She carried a cardboard suitcase and—believe me—a small harp in a cracked waterproof. Her straight light-brown hair was brushed and brushed and grained with blondness and spread in a kind of cape over her shoulders. Her face seemed full and merry.

"Are you hitchhiking?" I asked.

"Yes."

"But isn't it dangerous for a girl your age?"

"Not at all."

"Do you travel much?"

"All the time. I sing a little. I play the coffeehouses."

"What do you sing?"

"Oh, folk music, mostly. And some old things—Purcell and Dowland. But mostly folk music. . . . 'I gave my love a cherry that had no stone,' " she sang in a true and pretty voice. " 'I gave my love a chicken that had no bone/I told my love a story that had no end/I gave my love a baby with no cryin'.' "

She sang me across a bridge that seemed to be an astonishingly sensible, durable, and even beautiful construction designed by intelligent men to simplify my travels, and the water of the Hudson below us was charming and tranquil. It all came back—blue-sky courage, the high spirits of lustiness, an ecstatic sereneness. Her song ended as we got to the toll station on the east bank, and she thanked me, said goodbye, and got out of the car. I offered to take her wherever she wanted to go, but she shook her head and walked away, and I drove on toward the city through a world that, having been restored to me, seemed marvelous and fair. When I got home, I thought of calling my brother and telling him what had happened, on the chance that there was also an angel of the elevator banks, but the harp—that single detail—threatened to make me seem ridiculous or mad, and I didn't call.

I wish I could say that I am convinced that there will always be some merciful intercession to help me with my worries, but I don't believe in pushing my luck, so I will stay off the George Washington Bridge, although I can cross the Triborough and the Tappan Zee with ease. My brother is still afraid of elevators, and my mother, although she's grown quite stiff, still goes around and around and around on the ice.

My Guardian Angel Stein

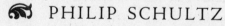 PHILIP SCHULTZ

In our house every floor was a wailing wall
& each sideward glance a history of insult.
Nightly Grandma bolted the doors believing God

had a personal grievance to settle on our heads.
Not Atreus exactly but we had furies (Uncle Jake
banged the tables demanding respect from fate) & enough

outrage to impress Aristotle with the prophetic unity
of our misfortune. No wonder I hid behind the sofa sketching
demons to identify the faces in my dreams & stayed under

bath water until my lungs split like pomegranate seeds.
Stein arrived one New Year's Eve fresh from a salvation in Budapest.
Nothing in his 6,000 years prepared him for our nightly bacchanal

of immigrant indignity except his stint in the Hundred Years' War
where he lost his eyesight & faith both. This myopic angel knew
everything about calamity (he taught King David the art of hubris

& Moses the price of fame) & quoted Dante to prove others
had it worse. On winter nights we memorized the Dead Sea Scrolls
until I could sleep without a night light & he explained why

the stars appear only at night ("Insomniacs, they study the Torah
all day!"). Once I asked him outright: "Stein, why is our house
so unhappy?" Adjusting his rimless glasses, he said: "Boychick,

life is a comedy salted with despair. All humans are disappointed.
Laugh yourself to sleep each night & with luck, pluck & credit cards
you'll beat them at their own game. Catharsis is necessary in this house!"

Ah, Stein, bless your outsized wings & balding pate & while I'm at it why not bless the imagination's lonely fray with time, which, yes, like love & family romance, has neither beginning, middle nor end.

PART THREE

Wrestling with Angels

To come to know an angel is not always simple. What happens if an angel's presence is disturbing or overwhelming? What if one yearns for a life untouched by angels? In the writings that follow, angels unnerve people. In presenting themselves, or in their announcements, they seem to intrude into people's lives, changing human life-stories in ways that are unanticipated and challenging. Sometimes the intrusion is profoundly physical: an angel burns the ear, breaks the eye, or enters the womb. Sometimes an angel seems to be so close that it becomes part of oneself; to wrestle with an angel, then, is to wrestle with oneself. From such a struggle, and such intimacy, one may gain something precious. Yet the questions that hover throughout so many of these pieces do not admit of easy resolutions: Who is this other with whom I am wrestling? And how do I know that what it brings is good?

Angel

JAMES MERRILL

Above my desk, whirring and self-important
(Though not much larger than a hummingbird)
In finely woven robes, school of Van Eyck,
Hovers a patently angelic visitor.
He points one index finger out the window
At winter snatching to its heart,
To crystal vacancy, the misty
Exhalations of houses and of people running home
From the cold sun pounding on the sea;
While with the other hand
He indicates the piano
Where the Sarabande No. 1 lies open
At a passage I shall never master
But which has already, and effortlessly, mastered me.
He drops his jaw as if to say, or sing,
"Between the world God made
And this music of Satie,
Each glimpsed through veils, but whole,
Radiant and willed,

Demanding praise, demanding surrender,
How can you sit there with your notebook?
What do you think you are doing?"
However he says nothing—wisely: I could mention
Flaws in God's world, or Satie's; and for that matter
How did he come by *his* taste for Satie?
Half to tease him, I turn back to my page,
Its phrases thus far clotted, unconnected.
The tiny angel shakes his head.
There is no smile on his round, hairless face.
He does not want even these few lines written.

Letter to "A"

 FLANNERY O'CONNOR

From *The Habit of Being*

I don't want to be any angel but my relations with them have improved over a period of time. They weren't always even speakable. I went to the Sisters to school for the first 6 years or so . . . at their hands I developed something the Freudians have not named—anti-angel aggression, call it. From 8 to 12 years it was my habit to seclude myself in a locked room every so often and with a fierce (and evil) face, whirl around in a circle with my fists knotted, socking the angel. This was the guardian angel with which the Sisters assured us we were all equipped. He never left you. My dislike of him was poisonous. I'm sure I even kicked at him and landed on the floor. You couldn't hurt an angel but I would have been happy to know I had dirtied his feathers—I conceived of him in feathers. Anyway, the Lord removed this fixation from me by His Merciful Kindness and I have not been troubled by it since. In fact I forgot that angels existed until a couple of years ago the *Catholic Worker* sent me a card on which was printed a prayer to St. Raphael ... The prayer asks St. Raphael to guide us to the province of joy so that we may not be ignorant of the concerns of our true country. All this led me to find out eventually what angels were, or anyway what they were not. And what they are not is a big comfort to me ...

Jacob Wrestles with an Angel

GENESIS 32:24–32

And Jacob was left alone; and a man wrestled with him until the breaking of the day. When the man saw that he did not prevail against Jacob, he touched the hollow of his thigh; and Jacob's thigh was put out of joint as he wrestled with him. Then he said, "Let me go, for the day is breaking." But Jacob said, "I will not let you go, unless you bless me." And he said to him, "What is your name?" And he said, "Jacob." Then he said, "Your name shall no more be called Jacob, but Israel, for you have striven with God and with men, and have prevailed." Then Jacob asked him, "Tell me, I pray, your name." But he said, "Why is it that you ask my name?" And there he blessed him. So Jacob called the name of the place Peni'el, saying, "For I have seen God face to face, and yet my life is preserved." The sun rose upon him as he passed Penu'el, limping because of his thigh. Therefore to this day the Israelites do not eat the sinew of the hip which is upon the hollow of the thigh, because he touched the hollow of Jacob's thigh on the sinew of the hip.

Lazar Malkin Enters Heaven

STEVE STERN

My father-in-law, Lazar Malkin, may he rest in peace, refused to die. This was in keeping with his lifelong stubbornness. Of course there were those who said that he'd passed away already and come back again, as if death were another of his so-called peddling trips, from which he always returned with a sackful of crazy gifts.

There were those in our neighborhood who joked that he'd been dead for years before his end. And there was more than a little truth in this. Hadn't he been declared clinically kaput not once but twice on the operating table? Over the years they'd extracted more of his internal organs than it seemed possible to do without. And what with his wooden leg, his empty left eye socket concealed by a gabardine patch, his missing teeth and sparse white hair, there was hardly enough of old Lazar left in this world to constitute a human being.

"Papa," my wife, Sophie, once asked him, just after the first of his miraculous recoveries, "what was it like to be dead?" She was sometimes untactful, my Sophie, and in this she took after her father—whose child she was by one of his unholy alliances. (Typically obstinate, he had always refused to marry.)

Lazar had looked at her with his good eye, which, despite being set in a face like last week's roast, was usually wet and amused.

"Why ask me?" he wondered, refusing to take the question seriously. "Ask Alabaster the cobbler, who ain't left his shop in fifty years. He makes shoes, you'd think he's building coffins. Ask Petrofsky whose lunch counter serves nobody but ghosts. Ask Gruber the shammes or Milstein the tinsmith. Ask your husband, who is as good as wearing his sewing machine around his neck . . ."

I protested that he was being unfair, though we both knew that he wasn't. The neighborhood, which was called the Pinch, had been dead since the War. Life and business had moved east, leaving us with our shops falling down around our ears. Myself and the others, we kidded ourselves that North Main Street would come back. Our children would come back again. The ready-made industry, we kept insisting, was just a passing fancy; people would return to quality. So who needed luftmenschen like Lazar to remind us that we were deceived?

"The Pinch ain't the world," he would inform us, before setting off on one of his mysterious peddling expeditions. He would haul himself into the cab of his corroded relic of a truck piled with shmattes and tools got on credit from a local wholesale outfit. Then he would sputter off in some random direction for points unknown.

Weeks later he would return, his pockets as empty as the bed of his truck. But he always brought back souvenirs in his burlap sack, which he prized like the kid in the story who swapped a cow for a handful of beans.

"I want you to have this," he would say to Mr. Alabaster or Gruber or Schloss or myself. Then he would give us a harp made out of a crocodile's tail; he would give us a Negro's toe, a root that looked like a little man, a contraption called a go-devil, a singletree, the uses of which he had no idea. "This will make you wise," he told us. "This will make you amorous. This came from Itta Bena and this from Nankipoo"—as if they were places as far away as China, which for all we knew they were.

"Don't thank me," he would say, like he thought we might be speechless with gratitude. Then he would borrow a few bucks and limp away to whatever hole in the wall he was staying in.

Most of my neighbors got rid of Lazar's fetishes and elixirs, complaining that it made them nervous to have them around. I was likewise inclined, but in deference to my wife I kept them. Rather than leave them lying around the apartment, however, I tossed them into the storage shed behind my shop.

•   •   •

No one knew how old Lazar really was, though it was generally agreed that he was far past the age when it was still dignified to be alive. None of us, after all, was a spring chicken anymore. We were worn out from the years of trying to supplement our pensions with the occasional alteration or the sale of a pair of shoelaces. If our time should be near, nobody was complaining. Funerals were anyhow the most festive occasions we had in the Pinch. We would make a day of it, traveling in a long entourage out to the cemetery, then back to North Main for a feast at the home of the bereaved. You might say that death was very popular in our neighborhood. So it aggravated us that Lazar, who preceded us by a whole generation, should persist in hanging around.

He made certain that most of what we knew about him was hearsay. It was his nature to be mysterious. Even Sophie, his daughter by one of his several scandals, knew only the rumors. As to the many versions of his past, she would tell me to take my pick. "I would rather not, if you don't mind," I said. The idea of Lazar Malkin as a figure of romance was a little more than I could handle. But that never stopped Sophie from regaling me by telling stories of her father the way another woman might sing to herself.

He lost his eye as a young man, when he refused to get out of the way of a rampaging Cossack in his village of Podolsk. Walking away from Kamchatka, where he'd been sent for refusing to be drafted into the army of the Czar, the frostbite turned to gangrene and he lost his leg. Or was it the other way around? He was dismembered by a Cossack, snowblinded in one eye for good? . . . What did it matter? The only moral I got out of the tales of Lazar's mishegoss was that every time he refused to do what was sensible, there was a little less of him left to refuse with.

It puzzled me that Sophie could continue to have such affection for the old kocker. Hadn't he ruined her mother, among others, at a time when women did not go so willingly to their ruin? Of course, the living proofs of his wickedness were gone now. His old mistresses had long since passed on, and it was assumed there were no offspring other than Sophie. Though sometimes I was haunted by the thought of the surrounding countryside populated by the children of Lazar Malkin.

So what was the attraction? Did the ladies think he was some pirate with his eye patch and clunking artificial leg? That one I still find hard to swallow. Or maybe they thought that with him it didn't count. Because he refused to settle down to any particular life, it was as if he had no legitimate life at all. None worth considering in any case. And I cursed myself for the time I took to think about him, an old fool responsible for making my wife a bastard—though who could think of Sophie in such a light?

· · ·

"You're a sick man, Lazar," I told him, meaning in more ways than one. "See a doctor."

"I never felt better, I'll dance on your grave," he insisted, asking me incidentally did I have a little change to spare.

I admit that this did not sit well with me, the idea of his hobbling a jig on my headstone. Lie down already and die, I thought, God forgive me. But from the way he'd been lingering in the neighborhood lately, postponing his journeys, it was apparent to whoever noticed that something was wrong. His unshaven face was the gray of dirty sheets, and his wizened stick of a frame was shrinking visibly. His odor, no longer merely the ripe stench of the unwashed, had about it a musty smell of decay. Despite my imploring, he refused to see a physician, though it wasn't like he hadn't been in the hospital before. (Didn't I have a bundle of his unpaid bills to prove it?) So maybe this time he knew that for what he had there wasn't a cure.

When I didn't see him for a while, I supposed that, regardless of the pain he was in, he had gone off on another of his peddling trips.

"Your father needs a doctor," I informed Sophie over dinner one night.

"He won't go," she said, wagging her chins like what can you do with such a man. "So I invited him to come stay with us."

She offered me more kreplach, as if my wide-open mouth meant that I must still be hungry. I was thinking of the times he'd sat at our table in the vile, moth-eaten overcoat he wore in all seasons. I was thinking of the dubious mementos he left us with.

"Don't worry," said my good wife, "he won't stay in the apartment . . ."

"Thank God."

". . . But he asked if he could have the shed out back."

"I won't have it!" I shouted, putting my foot down. "I won't have him making a flophouse out of my storehouse."

"Julius," said Sophie in her watch-your-blood-pressure tone of voice, "he's been out there a week already."

I went down to the little brick shed behind the shop. The truth was that I seldom used it—only to dump the odd bolt of material and the broken sewing machines that I was too attached to to throw away. And Lazar's gifts. Though I could see through the window that an oil lamp was burning beneath a halo of mosquitoes, there was no answer to my knock. Entering anyway, I saw cobwebs, mouse droppings, the usual junk—but no Lazar.

Then I was aware of him propped in a chair in a corner, his burlap sack and a few greasy dishes at his feet. It took me so long to notice because I was not used to seeing him sit still. Always he was hopping from his real leg to his phony, being a nuisance, telling us we ought to get out and see more of the world. Now with his leg unhitched and lying across some skeins of mildewed cloth, I could have mistaken him for one of my discarded manikins.

"Lazar," I said, "in hospitals they at least have beds."

"Who sleeps?" he wanted to know, his voice straining up from his hollow chest. This was as much as admitting his frailty. Shocked out of my aggravation, I proceeded to worry.

"You can't live in here," I told him, thinking that no one would confuse this with living. "Pardon my saying so, but it stinks like Gehinom." I had observed the coffee tin he was using for a slop jar.

"A couple of days," he managed in a pathetic attempt to recover his native chutzpah, "and I'll be back on my feet again. I'll hit the road." When he coughed, there was dust, like when you beat a rug.

I looked over at one of the feet that he hoped to be back on and groaned. It might have been another of his curiosities, taking its place alongside of the boar's tusk and the cypress knee.

"Lazar," I implored, astonished at my presumption, "go to heaven already. Your organs and limbs are waiting there for a happy reunion. What do you want to hang around this miserable place for anyway?" I made a gesture intended to take in more than the shed, which included the whole of the dilapidated Pinch with its empty shops and abandoned synagogue. Then I understood that for Lazar my gesture had included even more. It took in the high roads to Iuka and Yazoo City, where the shwartzers swapped him moonshine for a yard of calico.

"Heaven," he said in a whisper that was half a shout, turning his head to spit on the floor. "Heaven is wasted on the dead. Anyway, I like it here."

Feeling that my aggravation had returned, I started to leave.

"Julius," he called to me, reaching into the sack at his feet, extracting with his withered fingers I don't know what—some disgusting composition of feathers and bones and hair. "Julius," he wheezed in all sincerity, "I have something for you."

What can you do with such a man?

. . .

I went back the following afternoon with Dr. Seligman. Lazar told the doctor don't touch him, and the doctor shrugged like he didn't need to dirty his hands.

"Malkin," he said, "this isn't becoming. You can't borrow time the way you borrow gelt."

Seligman was something of a neighborhood philosopher. Outside the shed he assured me that the old man was past worrying about. "If he thinks he can play hide-and-go-seek with death, then let him. It doesn't hurt anybody but himself." He had such a way of putting things, Seligman.

"But Doc," I said, still not comforted, "it ain't in *your* backyard that he's playing his farkokte game."

It didn't help, now that the word was out, that my so-called friends and neighbors treated me like I was confining old Lazar against his will. For years they'd wished him out of their hair, and now they behaved as if they actually missed him. Nothing was the same since he failed to turn up at odd hours in their shops, leaving them with some ugly doll made from corn husks or a rabbit's foot.

"You think I like it," I asked them, "that the old fortz won't get it over with?" Then they looked at me like it wasn't nice to take his name in vain.

Meanwhile Sophie continued to carry her noodle puddings and bowls of chicken broth out to the shed. She was furtive in this activity, as if she was harboring an outlaw, and sometimes I thought she enjoyed the intrigue. More often than not, however, she brought back her plates with the food untouched.

I still looked in on him every couple of days, though it made me nauseous. It spoiled my constitution, the sight of him practically decomposing.

"You're sitting shivah for yourself, that's what," I accused him, holding my nose. When he bothered to communicate, it was only in grunts.

I complained to Sophie: "I was worried a flophouse, but charnel house is more like it."

"Shah!" she said, like it mattered whether the old so-and-so could hear us. "Soon he'll be himself again."

I couldn't believe my ears.

"Petrofsky," I confided at his lunch counter the next day, "my wife's as crazy as Lazar. She thinks he's going to get well."

"So why you got to bury him before his time?"

Petrofsky wasn't the only one to express this sentiment. It was contagious. Alabaster, Ridblatt, Schloss, they were all in the act, all of them suddenly defenders of my undying father-in-law. If I so much as opened my mouth to kvetch about the old man, they told me hush up, they spat against the evil eye. "But only yesterday you said it's unnatural he should live so long," I protested.

"Doc," I told Seligman in the office where he sat in front of a standing skeleton, "the whole street's gone crazy. They think that maybe a one-legged corpse can dance again."

The doctor looked a little nervous himself, like somebody might be listening. He took off his nickel-rimmed spectacles to speak.

"Maybe they think that if the angel of death can pass over Lazar, he can pass over the whole neighborhood."

"Forgive me, Doctor, but you're crazy too. Since when is everyone so excited to preserve our picturesque community? And anyway, wouldn't your angel look first in an open grave, which after all is what the Pinch has become." Then I was angry with myself for having stooped to speaking in riddles too.

But in the end I began to succumb to the general contagion. I was afraid for Lazar, I told myself, though—who was I kidding?—like the rest, I was afraid for myself.

"Sophie," I confessed to my wife, who had been treating me like a stranger lately, "I wish that old Lazar was out peddling again." Without him out wandering in the boondocks beyond our neighborhood, returning with his cockamamie gifts, it was like there wasn't a "beyond" anymore. The Pinch, for better or worse, was all there was. This I tried to explain to my Sophie, who squeezed my hand like I was her Julius again.

.   .   .

Each time I looked in on him, it was harder to distinguish the immobile Lazar from the rest of the dust and drek. I described this to Seligman, expecting medical opinion, and got only that it put him in mind of the story of the golem—dormant and moldering in a synagogue attic these six hundred years.

Then there was a new development. There were bits of cloth sticking out of the old man's nostrils and ears, and he refused to open his mouth at all.

"It's to keep his soul from escaping," Sophie told me, mussing my hair as if any ninny could see that. I groaned and rested my head in my hands, trying not to imagine what other orifices he might have plugged up.

After that I didn't visit him anymore. I learned to ignore Sophie, with her kerchief over her face against the smell, going to and fro with the food he refused to eat. I was satisfied it was impossible that he should still be alive, which fact made it easier to forget about him for periods of time.

This was also the tack that my friends and neighbors seemed to be taking. On the subject of Lazar Malkin we had all become deaf and dumb. It was like he was a secret we shared, holding our breaths lest someone should find us out.

Meanwhile on North Main Street it was business (or lack of same) as usual.

Of course I wasn't sleeping so well. In the middle of the night I remembered that, among the items and artifacts stored away in my shed, there was my still breathing father-in-law. This always gave an unpleasant jolt to my system. Then I would get out of bed and make what I called my cocktail—some antacid and a shpritz of soda water. It was summer and the rooms above the shop were an oven, so I would go out to the open back porch for air. I would sip my medicine, looking down at the yard and the shed—where Lazar's lamp had not been kindled for a while.

On one such night, however, I observed that the lamp was burning again. What's more, I detected movement through the little window. Who knew but some miracle had taken place and Lazar was up again? Shivering despite the heat, I grabbed my bathrobe and went down to investigate.

I tiptoed out to the shed, pressed my nose against the filthy windowpane, and told myself that I didn't see what I saw. But while I bit the heel of my hand to keep from crying out loud, he wouldn't go away—the stoop-shouldered man in his middle years, his face sad and creased like the seat of someone's baggy pants. He was wearing a rumpled blue serge suit, its coat a few sizes large to accommodate the hump on his back. Because it fidgeted and twitched, I thought at first that the hump must be alive; then I understood that it was a hidden pair of wings.

So this was he, Malach ha-Mavet, the Angel of Death. I admit to being somewhat disappointed. Such a sight should have been forbidden me, it should have struck me blind and left me gibbering in awe. But all I could feel for the angel's presence was my profoundest sympathy. The poor shnook, he obviously had his work cut out for him. From the way he massaged his temples with the tips of his fingers, his complexion a little bilious (from the smell?), I guessed that he'd been at it for a while. He looked like he'd come a long way expecting more cooperation than this.

"For the last time, Malkin," I could hear him saying, his tone quite similar in its aggravation to the one I'd used with Lazar myself, "are you or aren't you going to give up the ghost?"

In his corner old Lazar was nothing, a heap of dust, his moldy overcoat and eye patch the only indications that he was supposed to resemble a man.

"What are you playing, you ain't at home?" the angel went on. "You're at home. So who do you think you're fooling?"

But no matter how much the angel sighed like he didn't have all night, like the jig was already up, Lazar Malkin kept mum. For this I gave thanks and wondered how, in my moment of weakness, I had been on the side of the angel.

"Awright, awright," the angel was saying, bending his head to squeeze the bridge of his nose. The flame of the lamp leaped with every tired syllable he uttered. "So it ain't vested in me, the authority to take from you what you won't give. So what. I got my orders to bring you back. And if you don't come dead, I take you alive."

There was a stirring in Lazar's corner. Keep still, you fool, I wanted to say. But bony fingers had already emerged from his coatsleeves; they were snatching the plugs of cloth from his ears. The angel leaned forward as if Lazar had spoken, but I could hear nothing—oh, maybe a squeak like a rusty hinge. Then I heard it again.

"Nu?" was what Lazar had said.

The angel began to repeat the part about taking him back, but before he could finish, Lazar interrupted.

"Take me where?"

"Where else?" said the angel. "To paradise, of course."

There was a tremor in the corner which produced a commotion of moths.

"Don't make me laugh," the old man replied, actually coughing the distant relation of a chortle. "There ain't no such place."

The angel: "I beg your pardon?"

"You heard me," said Lazar, his voice became amazingly clear.

"Okay," said the angel, trying hard not to seem offended. "We're even. In paradise they'll never believe you're for real."

Where he got the strength then I don't know—unless it was born from the pain that he'd kept to himself all those weeks—but Lazar began to get up. Spider webs came apart and bugs abandoned him like he was sprouting out of the ground. Risen to his foot, he cried out,

"There ain't no world but this!"

The flame leaped, the windowpane rattled.

This was apparently the final straw. The angel shook his melancholy head, mourning the loss of his patience. He removed his coat, revealing a sweat-stained shirt and a pitiful pair of wings no larger than a chicken's.

"Understand, this is not my style," he protested, folding his coat, approaching what was left of my father-in-law.

Lazar dropped back into the chair, which collapsed beneath him. When the angel attempted to pull him erect, he struggled. I worried a moment that the old man might crumble to pieces in the angel's embrace. But he was substantial enough to shriek bloody murder, and not too proud to offer bribes: "I got for you a nice feather headdress . . ."

He flopped about and kicked as the angel stuffed him head first into his own empty burlap peddler's sack.

Then the worldweary angel manhandled Lazar—whose muffled voice was still trying to bargain from inside his sack—across the cluttered shed. And hefting his armload, the angel of death battered open the back door, then carried his burden, still kicking, over the threshold.

I threw up the window sash and opened my mouth to shout. But I never found my tongue. Because that was when, before the door slammed behind them, I got a glimpse of kingdom come.

It looked exactly like the yard in back of the shop, only—how should I explain it?—sensitive. It was the same brick wall with glass embedded on top, the same ashes and rusty tin cans, but they were tender and ticklish to look at. Intimate like (excuse me) flesh beneath underwear. For the split second that the door stayed open, I felt that I was turned inside-out, and what I saw was glowing under my skin in place of my kishkes and heart.

Wiping my eyes, I hurried into the shed and opened the back door. What met me was a wall, some ashes and cans, some unruly weeds and vines, the rear of the derelict coffee factory, the rotten wooden porches of the tenements of our dreary neighborhood. Then I remembered—slapping my forehead, stepping gingerly into the yard—that the shed had never had a back door.

· · ·

Climbing the stairs to our apartment, I had to laugh out loud.

"Sophie!" I shouted to my wife—who, without waking, told me where to find the bicarbonate of soda. "Sophie," I cried, "set a place at the table for your father. He'll be coming back with God only knows what souvenirs."

From *Angel*

 HAROLD BRODKEY

Today The Angel of Silence and of Inspiration (toward Truth) appeared to a number of us passing by on the walk in front of Harvard Hall—this was a little after three o'clock—today is October twenty-fifth, nineteen-hundred-and-fifty-one.

The shadow came first. In my case, I looked up to see if the sky had clouded over and saw instead with amazing shock the rudiments of a large face, not in any perspective, but a facelike thing that was also a figure, not with feet nearest me, then legs, and so on, and not frontal, but smoothly and yet crudely present in all the visual and mental ways figures and faces sometimes are for me in my dreams.

It was like the shifting sense of things in dreams, seen and known in varied ways; and what was paramount was an observing—and kind but not forward—*facedness*, a prow of knowing making Itself known—a Countenance, not human, not exactly—or entirely—inhuman, conceivably human in relation, but one that did not suggest It ever knew unconsciousness or error—or slyness—and I was startled but not made insane but was studentlike—but not at once awed into complete readiness to be changed in every part of myself, but that came within seconds, as the world, the visible bricks and roofs, trees, leaves, people, lost color and shrank in scale—by comparison.

.   .   .

I confess I felt mostly shock and doubt; I was blinkingly, rebelliously, impiously, ineptly disrespectful and restless among moments of severe awe, even at first; I was withdrawn, then attentive, then withdrawn again differently. My attention, my attentiveness, my strained and straining openness, my aching openness, the struggle to be open with no self-defense, was not singlehearted—I resisted The Announcement, The Inspiration, The Angel, The Seraphic Messenger, not that I doubted that the soul (which is, in a way, the whole of what we have done in the light of what has been done to us) in its distances of belief—philosophy and awe—was at bottom *childlike-and-pious* but I could ignore the child in me to some extent even when, if I may be permitted to say this, God in this form faced me.

The Great Seraph did not seem to be, in any sense, *militant*—not the least *military*—or, for that matter, musical, either. It was neither distant nor fond, It was not commanding or alluring; the phenomenon of Itself was of rare abilities on a not-human base—but related—compacted here into a somewhat recognizable Figure—somewhat recognizable—considerably larger than I was, more undeniably fine than anything I had ever seen, more conscious, but oddly in a way, so that I do not know and I did not know then, I did not know and I had no continuous faith, no conviction about what It was conscious of—love, say, or distant patience, or what. I was aware even then that others saw It differently—as Patience, say, or as Love, or as Militance—but to me It signified nothing, not even the degree to which It was willful and what It might or might not do or say: It represented only Beauty and Meaning, which is to say Truth, but not my truth so far, which is to say, then, New Truth—ungraspable at first, and perhaps always—and It was partly Old Truth, from which I had strayed—but Truth would always be so new, as new as This Figure was, that one might then be slightly—or even strongly—driven to slighting behavior toward It as a result.

Impiety. Self-defense. Rebellion. Whatever.

Those were clearer to me—those modes of resistance—than was the terror of what Acceptance would bring.

It seems to me now it was impiety or selfishness on my part to think that except as the end of things It was not otherwise humanly relevant. It was relevant at its own say-so.

I noticed that It seemed to be overwhelmingly *suitable*—I wanted suddenly to be like It; this struck me at the second I felt it, this desire, as it formed, that it was now the supreme fact of my life, this aesthetic, this being influenced by a function of The Angel's quality—this was *Love*, I presume, for an apparition, one that affected my senses, a reality, an appearance.

The absence of vengeance in Its stance and Its being without any of the accoutrements of myth—It carried no symbols, It was dressed in nothing but undefinability, It was not dressed or undressed, It was not naked, It was neutrally and luminously clear and unclear—It was contentedly beyond the need of further signification—It would never be modified or added to, argued with, corrected, or moved—that is, It was post-Apocalyptic: I fell in love with It as *The End and Be-All*; I fell in love with silence—Its silence anyway.

But the mind, bemused or sanctified or not, in love and a-soar and wishing to be obedient, does not cease to feel and wobble—wobble means think—it discards thoughts and feelings as they draw notice, as they appear they are dismissed. But still one's heart vibrates, too, between attention and inattention, or rather between low desire—physical desire—and a wish *consciously* (i.e., sinlessly) to know—without physical will—but one gives in to physical desire anyway as feeling if not as act: I did not walk toward The Angel—not more than a few feet, if that; perhaps I imagined it. I expired in a kind of light. The Angel was suitable and I was not, but I imagined an embrace, my will having its way with this Lighted *suitability* that had altered history and was altering it now, without apparently being altered by any of this. *My God, my God.* I thought The Angel had ended history. I thought I ought to walk in The White Furnace of Its Glory—The Grand Wars of God, The Chambers of Holocaust—Daniel and Joseph—I don't know what my ego and heart and soul were thinking of—It was there, The Angel, and merely in Its being present, It made it stupid to lie; and this was so whether It was an Angel or a hoax, or rather It could not be a use-less hoax since It was authentically, irregularly, idiosyncratically joy and awe and so summoning and wonderful in Its form. I longed to know how the others there felt This Apparition, but it seemed pointless finally since our opinions did not matter, and since so long as It was present we were not commanded by ourselves, by our opinions, or by each other but only by It, Its presence. It hadn't oc-curred to me before this moment that ours was a species of habitual judgment, but now that this faculty of conscious mind was useless—assent and praise were hardly required—I did think, with some unclarity, that Judgment Day, like now, would be an occasion of the banishing of judgment from us. This seemed tremendously sexual. It was awful to know my life had to change beyond my power to influence or judge or analyze or find Reason—I could not limit the new consciousness except by unconsciousness, by fainting. Mind would change in the light of Possibility inherent in the fact of The Seen Angel—Its Goodness, Its Forbearance: It did NO HUMAN THING. We saw This Angel and It did nothing, This Particular One, Its Appearance, It was one Angel and not an *example* of any-thing—it could not be multiplied or divided—by us, by our minds, by mine. It was *a Thing*, a kind of Silent Goodness, but not an ex-ample. To be governed by Revelation in this form is a tremendous thing and unmanning, much as when a woman says, *All right, I will tell you a truth or two*, and she means it as an act of rule, and what she then says does affect you; if it does, if the revelation changes the way you think, it does make you crazed and weak, perhaps: you are in an unknown place or facet of consciousness: It was like this but much, much, much more so. It was at this point that I went down on my knees and then, after a second, rose again, choosing to stand

in the face of This Androgynous Power, which being of this order
of magnitude and of this maternal a quality yet seemed male to me.

Of course, It was perceived by others according to different bodies
of symbols derived from their lives and dreams—and they saw It as
warlike or virgin-maidenly, or virgin-maidenly and warlike, or as like
a father, and not at all in the way that I saw It. For some, It was Pure
Voice and Radiance and not a figure at all, but for everyone I spoke
to or looked at, It was Actuality—and It could be ignored or inter-
preted as one liked but only at one's peril: that was admitted.

to joan

 LUCILLE CLIFTON

joan
did you never hear
in the soft rushes of france
merely the whisper of french grass
rubbing against leathern
sounding now like a windsong
now like a man?
did you never wonder
oh fantastical joan,
did you never cry in the sun's face
unreal   unreal? did you never run
villageward
hands pushed out toward your apron?

and just as you knew that your mystery
was broken for all time
did they not fall then
soft as always
into your ear
calling themselves michael
among beloved others?
and you
sister   sister
did you not then sigh
my voices   my voices   of course?

The Evil Angel

✿ HOWARD SCHWARTZ

The head of a yeshiva had a daughter who was modest and virtuous, and he sought to find a suitable match for her. Now among the students at his yeshiva was a young scholar who was filled with the fear of heaven. He devoted himself to the study of Torah day and night; he even awoke at midnight to continue his studies. The head of the yeshiva realized that this young man, who came from a fine family, would make an ideal son-in-law.

He proposed the match to the young man's family, and they were delighted to approve it, as was the young man himself, who had the highest respect for the *rosh yeshiva*. A fine wedding was held, and after the wedding the head of the yeshiva made it possible for the groom to devote himself completely to the Torah. So it was that in time the young man became a master of the Torah and achieved a high level of holiness.

One night, while the young man was alone in the House of Study, a light suddenly filled the room, and when he looked up he saw an angelic presence. The angel explained that it had descended from on high to teach him the Torah of the angels. And before it departed at dawn, the angel revealed secrets of the Torah that the young man had never even imagined.

Now the young man knew that an angel sometimes descends to this world to serve as a *maggid*, an angelic teacher. This had happened with Joseph Caro and a handful of other great sages, and the young man was thrilled that such an angel should seek him out. At the same time, he was very modest and dared not reveal such a thing to anyone, not even to his wife or his father-in-law.

After that the angel returned to the young student only late at night, when he was alone in the House of Study. There the angel continued to reveal mysteries that are only known on high.

Then one night the student asked the angel a question, and the angel refused to reply. What the young man wanted to know, the angel said, could force the coming of the Messiah. Now that is what the student longed for more than anything else, and night after night he begged the *maggid* to share this powerful secret, but the angel continued to refuse.

The young man tried every way he could think of to extract this secret from the angel, but without success. At last the angel agreed to reveal it if he would first obey a single request. The young man was ready to do anything, until he learned that the angel wanted him to commit a sin.

The young man was thrown into great confusion. He struggled with himself and told the angel that he would have to think the matter over. In the following days he continued to resist the sin, but at the same time his longing to know the secret grew even greater. At last he confided his confusion to his wife, who could barely believe what her husband told her and was appalled by the sin that the angel had called on him to commit.

She, in turn, went to her father and asked for his help. He was shocked at what she told him and saw that his son-in-law was in great danger. He went to see the young man at once and told him that he knew his secret. Then the *rosh yeshiva* explained that there are two kinds of angels, those from the Side of Holiness and those from the *Sitre Ahre*, the Other Side. How could they be distinguished? By the appearance of the Name of God on their foreheads. For God's Name is written on the forehead of every kind of angel, but in the case of the angels from the Side of Holiness, the Name burns like a white flame, while on the angels from the Other Side it is inscribed in a black flame. He asked the young man which kind of angel it was, but the young man was not certain, for he had not dared to look at the angel's face.

Then the head of the yeshiva told his son-in-law that the next time the angel came to him, he must find out the truth at once. And if it was an evil angel who had approached him—and surely it must be, for what other angel would call upon him to commit a sin?—he was in grave danger. He gave the young man a small round mirror and told him to be sure to keep it with him at all times. And should he discover that it was indeed an evil angel, he must hold up the mirror before the angel at once.

Now the next time the angel came to visit, the young man looked carefully at its forehead, and he saw that the Name of God did glow darkly there, confirming that he had been led astray by an evil angel. The angel realized at once that the young man had perceived its true identity, and it was prepared to slay him, but the young man pulled out the mirror and held it before the angel's face. And when the angel saw its image reflected in that mirror, it was forced to confront its own evil nature, and in that instant it ceased to exist.

So it was that the young yeshiva student was saved from the evil angel, and he lived a long life filled with a love of Torah that he never lost. And never again did the forces of evil seek to seduce him with forbidden knowledge.

The Mother of God

 WILLIAM BUTLER YEATS

The threefold terror of love; a fallen flare
Through the hollow of an ear;
Wings beating about the room;
The terror of all terrors that I bore
The Heavens in my womb.

Had I not found content among the shows
Every common woman knows,
Chimney corner, garden walk,
Or rocky cistern where we tread the clothes
And gather all the talk?

What is this flesh I purchased with my pains,
This fallen star my milk sustains,
This love that makes my heart's blood stop
Or strikes a sudden chill into my bones
And bids my hair stand up?

mary's dream

 LUCILLE CLIFTON

winged women was saying
"full of grace" and like.
was light beyond sun and words
of a name and a blessing.
winged women to only i.
i joined them, whispering
yes.

holy night

 LUCILLE CLIFTON

joseph, i afraid of stars,
their brilliant seeing.
so many eyes. such light.

joseph, i cannot still these limbs,
i hands keep moving toward i breasts,
so many stars. so bright.
joseph, is wind burning from east
joseph, i shine, oh joseph,   oh
illuminated night.

island mary

 LUCILLE CLIFTON

after the all been done and i
one old creature carried on
another creature's back, i wonder
could i have fought these thing?
surrounded by no son of mine save
old men calling mother like in the tale
the astrologer tell, i wonder
could i have walk away when voices
singing in my sleep? i one old woman.
always i seem to worrying now for
another young girl asleep
in the plain evening.
what song around her ear?
what star still choosing?

Mary and Gabriel

THE KORAN

Relate in the book (that is, the Koran) the history of Mary, when she retired from her family to a place towards the east, in the house, and she took a veil to conceal herself from them; and We sent unto her our spirit Gabriel, and he appeared unto her as a perfect man. She said, I beg the Compassionate to preserve me from thee! If thou be a pious person, thou wilt withdraw from me.—He replied, I am only the messenger of thy Lord to inform thee that He will give thee a pure son, endowed with the gift of prophecy. She said, How shall I have a son, when a man hath not touched me, and I am not a harlot? He answered, Thus shall it be: a son shall be created unto thee without a father. Thy Lord saith, This is easy unto Me; and thus shall it be that We may make him a sign unto men, showing Our power, and a mercy from Us unto him who shall believe in him: for it is a thing decreed.—And she conceived him; and she retired with him yet unborn to a distant place far from her family; and the pains of childbirth urged her to repair to the trunk of a palm-tree that she might lean against it. And she gave birth to the child, which was conceived and formed and born in an hour. She said, Oh! would that I had died before this event, and had been a thing forgotten and unnoticed!—But he who was below her (namely Gabriel, who was on a lower place than she) called to her, Grieve not. God hath made below thee a rivulet: and shake thou towards thee the trunk of the palm-tree (which was dried-up); it shall let fall upon thee ripe dates, fresh-gathered: therefore eat of the dates, and drink of the water of the rivulet, and be of cheerful eye on account

A place to stand and love in for a day,
With darkness and the death-hour rounding it.

From *Professions for Women**

 VIRGINIA WOOLF

When your secretary invited me to come here, she told me that your Society is concerned with the employment of women and she suggested that I might tell you something about my own professional experiences. It is true I am a woman; it is true I am employed; but what professional experiences have I had? It is difficult to say. My profession is literature; and in that profession there are fewer experiences for women than in any other, with the exception of the stage—fewer, I mean, that are peculiar to women. For the road was cut many years ago—by Fanny Burney, by Aphra Behn, by Harriet Martineau, by Jane Austen, by George Eliot—many famous women, and many more unknown and forgotten, have been before me, making the path smooth, and regulating my steps. Thus, when I came to write, there were very few material obstacles in my way. Writing was a reputable and harmless occupation. The family peace was not broken by the scratching of a pen. No demand was made upon the family purse. For ten and sixpence one can buy paper enough to write all the plays of Shakespeare—if one has a mind that

*A paper read to The Women's Service League.

way. Pianos and models, Paris, Vienna and Berlin, masters and mistresses, are not needed by a writer. The cheapness of writing paper is, of course, the reason why women have succeeded as writers before they have succeeded in the other professions.

But to tell you my story—it is a simple one. You have only got to figure to yourselves a girl in a bedroom with a pen in her hand. She had only to move that pen from left to right—from ten o'clock to one. Then it occurred to her to do what is simple and cheap enough after all—to slip a few of those pages into an envelope, fix a penny stamp in the corner, and drop the envelope into the red box at the corner. It was thus that I became a journalist; and my effort was rewarded on the first day of the following month—a very glorious day it was for me—by a letter from an editor containing a cheque for one pound ten shillings and sixpence. But to show you how little I deserve to be called a professional woman, how little I know of the struggles and difficulties of such lives, I have to admit that instead of spending that sum upon bread and butter, rent, shoes and stockings, or butcher's bills, I went out and bought a cat—a beautiful cat, a Persian cat, which very soon involved me in bitter disputes with my neighbours.

What could be easier than to write articles and to buy Persian cats with the profits? But wait a moment. Articles have to be about something. Mine, I seem to remember, was about a novel by a famous man. And while I was writing this review, I discovered that if I were going to review books I should need to do battle with a certain phantom. And the phantom was a woman, and when I came to know her better I called her after the heroine of a famous poem, The Angel in the House. It was she who used to come between me and my paper when I was writing reviews. It was she who bothered

me and wasted my time and so tormented me that at last I killed
her. You who come of a younger and happier generation may not
have heard of her—you may not know what I mean by the Angel
in the House. I will describe her as shortly as I can. She was intensely sympathetic. She was immensely charming. She was utterly
unselfish. She excelled in the difficult arts of family life. She sacri-
ficed herself daily. If there was chicken, she took the leg; if there
was a draught she sat in it—in short she was so constituted that she
never had a mind or a wish of her own, but preferred to sympa-
thize always with the minds and wishes of others. Above all—I need
not say it—she was pure. Her purity was supposed to be her chief
beauty—her blushes, her great grace. In those days—the last of
Queen Victoria—every house had its Angel. And when I came to
write I encountered her with the very first words. The shadow of
her wings fell on my page; I heard the rustling of her skirts in the
room. Directly, that is to say, I took my pen in my hand to review
that novel by a famous man, she slipped behind me and whispered:
'My dear, you are a young woman. You are writing about a book
that has been written by a man. Be sympathetic; be tender; flatter;
deceive; use all the arts and wiles of our sex. Never let anybody
guess that you have a mind of your own. Above all, be pure.' And
she made as if to guide my pen. I now record the one act for which
I take some credit to myself, though the credit rightly belongs to
some excellent ancestors of mine who left me a certain sum of
money—shall we say five hundred pounds a year?—so that it was
not necessary for me to depend solely on charm for my living. I
turned upon her and caught her by the throat. I did my best to kill
her. My excuse, if I were to be had up in a court of law, would be
that I acted in self-defence. Had I not killed her she would have

killed me. She would have plucked the heart out of my writing. For, as I found, directly I put pen to paper, you cannot review even a novel without having a mind of your own, without expressing what you think to be the truth about human relations, morality, sex. And all these questions, according to the Angel of the House, cannot be dealt with freely and openly by women; they must charm, they must conciliate, they must—to put it bluntly—tell lies if they are to succeed. Thus, whenever I felt the shadow of her wing or the radiance of her halo upon my page, I took up the inkpot and flung it at her. She died hard. Her fictitious nature was of great assistance to her. It is far harder to kill a phantom than a reality. She was always creeping back when I thought I had despatched her. Though I flatter myself that I killed her in the end, the struggle was severe; it took much time that had better have been spent upon learning Greek grammar; or in roaming the world in search of adventures. But it was a real experience; it was an experience that was bound to befall all women writers at that time. Killing the Angel in the House was part of the occupation of a woman writer.

Questions About Angels

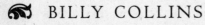 BILLY COLLINS

Of all the questions you might want to ask
about angels, the only one you ever hear
is how many can dance on the head of a pin.

No curiosity about how they pass the eternal time
besides circling the Throne chanting in Latin
or delivering a crust of bread to a hermit on earth
or guiding a boy and girl across a rickety wooden bridge.

Do they fly through God's body and come out singing?
Do they swing like children from the hinges
of the spirit world saying their names backwards and forwards?
Do they sit alone in little gardens changing colors?

What about their sleeping habits, the fabric of their robes,
their diet of unfiltered divine light?
What goes on inside their luminous heads? Is there a wall
these tall presences can look over and see hell?

If an angel fell off a cloud would he leave a hole
in a river and would the hole float along endlessly
filled with the silent letters of every angelic word?

If an angel delivered the mail would he arrive
in a blinding rush of wings or would he just assume
the appearance of the regular mailman and
whistle up the driveway reading the postcards?

No, the medieval theologians control the court.
The only question you ever hear is about
the little dance floor on the head of a pin
where halos are meant to converge and drift invisibly.

It is designed to make us think in millions,
billions, to make us run out of numbers and collapse
into infinity, but perhaps the answer is simply one:
one female angel dancing alone in her stocking feet,
a small jazz combo working in the background.

She sways like a branch in the wind, her beautiful
eyes closed, and the tall thin bassist leans over
to glance at his watch because she has been dancing
forever, and now it is very late, even for musicians.

PART FOUR

Angels in Difficulty

One of the questions rarely asked is this: How do angels feel? We think of angels as joyous and wise beings, filled with the presence of God, and we assume they are free of troubles. To imagine what character an angel would have, and all the turmoil and upheaval of an emotional life, catapults such a figure out of a perfect heaven and into an experience poignantly similar to our own. In the following stories and poems, angels can feel as powerless, and disappointed, as people. Often, they are disappointed in people, who treat these figures with remarkable cruelty and misunderstanding. Although for many of these human characters, love for another—even for an angel—is not possible, the writers suggest an alternative: our knowledge of ourselves and of God can grow with our openness to these humanly divine and divinely human figures.

The Guardian Angel

STEPHEN DUNN

Afloat between lives and stale truths,
   he realizes
he's never truly protected one soul,

they all die anyway, and what good
   is solace,
solace is cheap. The signs are clear:

the drooping wings, the shameless thinking
   about utility
and self. It's time to stop.

The guardian angel lives for a month
   with other angels,
sings the angelic songs, is reminded

that he doesn't have a human choice.
   The angel of love
lies down with him, and loving

restores to him his pure heart.
   Yet how hard it is
to descend into sadness once more.

When the poor are evicted, he stands
   between them
and the bank, but the bank sees nothing

in its way. When the meek are overpowered
   he's there, the thin air
through which they fall. Without effect

he keeps getting in the way of insults.
   He keeps wrapping
his wings around those in the cold.

Even his lamentations are unheard,
   though now,
in for the long haul, trying to live

beyond despair, he believes, he needs
   to believe
everything he does takes root, hums

beneath the surfaces of the world.

On Angels

DONALD BARTHELME

The death of God left the angels in a strange position. They were overtaken suddenly by a fundamental question. One can attempt to imagine the moment. How did they *look* at the instant the question invaded them, flooding the angelic consciousness, taking hold with terrifying force? The question was, "What are angels?"

New to questioning, unaccustomed to terror, unskilled in aloneness, the angels (we assume) fell into despair.

The question of what angels "are" has a considerable history. Swedenborg, for example, talked to a great many angels and faithfully recorded what they told him. Angels look like human beings, Swedenborg says. "That angels are human forms, or men, has been seen by me a thousand times." And again: "From all of my experience, which is now of many years, I am able to state that angels are wholly men in form, having faces, eyes, ears, bodies, arms, hands, and feet . . ." But a man cannot see angels with his bodily eyes, only with the eyes of the spirit.

Swedenborg has a great deal more to say about angels, all of the highest interest: that no angel is ever permitted to stand behind another and look at the back of his head, for this would disturb the influx of good and truth from the Lord; that angels have the east, where the Lord is seen as a sun, always before their eyes; and that angels are clothed according to their intelligence. "Some of the most intelligent have garments that blaze as if with flame, others have garments that glisten as if with light; the less intelligent have garments that are glistening white or white without the effulgence; and the still less intelligent have garments of various colors. But the angels of the inmost heaven are not clothed."

All of this (presumably) no longer obtains.

Gustav Davidson, in his useful *Dictionary of Angels*, has brought together much of what is known about them. Their names are called: the angel Elubatel, the angel Friagne, the angel Gaap, the angel Hatiphas (genius of finery), the angel Murmur (a fallen angel), the angel Mqttro, the angel Or, the angel Rash, the angel Sandalphon (taller than a five hundred years' journey on foot), the angel Smat. Davidson distinguishes categories: Angels of Quaking, who surround the heavenly throne; Masters of Howling and Lords of Shouting, whose work is praise; messengers, mediators, watchers, warners. Davidson's *Dictionary* is a very large book; his bibliography lists more than eleven hundred items.

The former angelic consciousness has been most beautifully described by Joseph Lyons (in a paper titled *The Psychology of Angels*, published in 1957). Each angel, Lyons says, knows all that there is to know about himself and every other angel. "No angel could ever ask a question, because questioning proceeds out of a situation of not knowing, and of being in some way aware of not knowing. An angel cannot be curious; he has nothing to be curious about. He cannot wonder. Knowing all that there is to know, the world of possible knowledge must appear to him as an ordered set of facts which is completely behind him, completely fixed and certain and within his grasp . . ."

But this, too, no longer obtains.

·   ·   ·

It is a curiosity of writing about angels that, very often, one turns out to be writing about men. The themes are twinned. Thus one finally learns that Lyons, for example, is really writing not about angels but about schizophrenics—thinking about men by invoking angels. And this holds true of much other writing on the subject—a point, we may assume, that was not lost on the angels when they began considering their new relation to the cosmos, when the analogues (is an angel more like a quetzal or more like a man? or more like music?) were being handed about.

We may further assume that some attempt was made at self-definition by function. An angel is what he does. Thus it was necessary to investigate possible new roles (you are reminded that this is impure speculation). After the lamentation had gone on for hundreds and hundreds of whatever the angels use for time, an angel proposed that lamentation be the function of angels eternally, as adoration was formerly. The mode of lamentation would be silence, in contrast to the unceasing chanting of Glorias that had been their former employment. But it is not in the nature of angels to be silent.

A counterproposal was that the angels affirm chaos. There were to be five great proofs of the existence of chaos, of which the first was the absence of God. The other four could surely be located. The work of definition and explication could, if done nicely enough, occupy the angels forever, as the contrary work has occupied human theologians. But there is not much enthusiasm for chaos among the angels.

The most serious because most radical proposal considered by the angels was refusal—that they would remove themselves from being, not be. The tremendous dignity that would accrue to the angels by this act was felt to be a manifestation of spiritual pride. Refusal was refused.

There were other suggestions, more subtle and complicated, less so, none overwhelmingly attractive.

I saw a famous angel on television; his garments glistened as if with light. He talked about the situation of angels now. Angels, he said, are like men *in some ways*. The problem of adoration is felt to be central. He said that for a time the angels had tried adoring each other, as we do, but had found it, finally, "not enough." He said they are continuing to search for a new principle.

The Vision of the Archangels

ᕰ RUPERT BROOKE

Slowly up silent peaks, the white edge of the world,
 Trod four archangels, clear against the unheeding sky,
Bearing, with quiet even steps, and great wings furled,
 A little dingy coffin; where a child must lie,
It was so tiny. (Yet, you had fancied, God could never
 Have bidden a child turn from the spring and the sunlight,
And shut him in that lonely shell, to drop for ever
 Into the emptiness and silence, into the night. : . .)

They then from the sheer summit cast, and watched it fall,
 Through unknown glooms, that frail black coffin—and therein
 God's little pitiful Body lying, worn and thin,
And curled up like some crumpled, lonely flower-petal—
Till it was no more visible; then turned again
With sorrowful quiet faces downward to the plain.

An Angel's Disquiet

❧ CLARICE LISPECTOR

Upon leaving the building, I was taken by surprise. What had been simply rain on the window-panes and been shut out by the curtains and cosy warmth indoors, was tempest and darkness outside on the street. Had this change taken place while I was going down in the lift? A Rio downpour without any shelter in sight. Copacabana with water seeping under the doorways of shops at street-level, thick muddy currents reaching half-way up my legs, as I probed with one foot to try and make contact with the invisible pavement. It was like an incoming tide which brought enough water in its wake to activate the moon's secret influence: there was already a tidal ebb and flow. Worst of all was that age-long fear engraved on the flesh: I am without shelter and the world has banished me to my own world. I, who can only be accommodated in a house, will never again possess a house. I am these soaking clothes. My drenched hair will never dry again, and I know that I shall not be among those destined to enter the Ark, for the best couple of my species has already been chosen.

On street-corners, cars have been abandoned, their engines para-lysed, and there is not a taxi in sight. The ferocious happiness of several man who find it impossible to return to their homes is un-mistakable. The diabolical happiness of men on the loose presented an even greater threat to a woman whose only desire was to return home as quickly as possible. I walked at random along street after street, dragging myself rather than walking: to stop, even for a second, would have meant danger. I barely managed to hide my overwhelming sense of desolation. Some fortunate soul under an improvised tent, called out: By jove, you're a courageous lady! It was not courage, it was definitely fear. Because everything was paralysed, I who am terrified of that moment in which everything comes to a standstill, felt I had to go on.

When suddenly, through the downpour, a taxi appeared. It advanced cautiously, moving centimetre by centimetre, as if testing the ground with its wheels. How was I to secure that taxi? I approached it. I could not afford the luxury of asking; I remembered all the times when, however sweetly I pleaded, my plea was refused. Suppressing my panic, which gave a false impression of strength, I said to the taxi-driver: "I must get home! it's late! I have small children who must be wondering where I am, it's already dark, do you hear me?" To my great surprise, the man simply answered: yes. Still puzzled, I got in. The taxi could scarcely move through the muddy currents, but it was moving—and it would eventually arrive. I was only thinking: this is more than I deserve. Soon I was thinking: it never occurred to me that I should be so deserving. And very soon, I was the mistress of my very own taxi. I had taken possession as if by right of something which had been given to me gratuitously, and I briskly set about tidying myself up: I wrung the water from my hair and clothes, pulled off my squelching shoes, and dried my face which looked tear-stained. I confess without shame that I had been weeping. Not much and for different reasons, but I had been weeping. After settling into my new domain, I leaned back comfortably in what was mine, and from my Ark, I watched the world come to an end.

Just then, a woman approached the car. As the taxi slowly ad-

vanced, she succeeded in accompanying it, holding on to the door-
handle in a state of distress. And she literally implored me to allow
her to share my taxi. I was already very late, and her route would
have meant making a lengthy detour. I remembered, however, my
own desperation five minutes earlier, and decided that she should
not suffer a similar crisis. When I said yes, her note of pleading immediately ceased, and was replaced with an extremely practical tone
of voice: "Good, but wait a minute while I go across the road to
collect a parcel which I left with the dressmaker so that it wouldn't
get soaked." "Is she taking advantage of me?" I asked myself in my
customary doubt as to whether I should or should not let people
take advantage of me. I ended up by giving in. The woman took her
time. And she came back carrying an enormous parcel which she
held on outstretched arms, as if contact with her own body might
stain the dress. She made herself comfortable on the back seat beside me, making me feel inhibited in my own home.

And my Calvary for being an angel began at once—for the
woman, with that authoritarian voice of hers, had already started to
call me an angel. Her situation could scarcely have been less endear-
ing: there was to be a *première* that night and, were it not for my
generosity, her dress would have been soaked in the rain or she
would have been late and missed the *première*. I had already experi-
enced my own *premières*, and had not been enthusiastic about any
of them. "You have no idea what a miracle this has been," she told
me firmly. "I started to pray in the street, to pray that God would
send an angel to my rescue; I made a vow that I would fast all day
tomorrow.—And God sent you." Feeling ill at ease, I fidgeted in my
seat. Was I an angel destined to salvage *premières*? The divine irony
left me disconcerted. But the woman, with all the force of her prac-

tical faith, and she was a forceful woman, vehemently insisted upon acknowledging me as an angel, something which very few people have ever acknowledged in the past, and even then with the greatest discretion. I tried to shrug it off with some mild sarcasm. "Don't over-estimate me, I am merely a means of transport." While she made no attempt to grasp my meaning, I unwillingly conceded that the argument did not really excuse me: angels are also a means of transport. Intimidated, I remained silent. I am always greatly impressed by anyone who shouts at me: the woman was not shouting, but she was clearly towering over me. Incapable of facing up to her, I took refuge in sweet cynicism: that woman who handled her own ecstasy with such vigour, must be a woman who was accustomed to paying with money, and almost certainly she would end up by rewarding her angel with a cheque, also bearing in mind that the rain must have washed away all my distinction. With a little more consoling cynicism, I silently informed her that money would be as legitimate a way as any other of thanking me, since her money was really money. Or—I thought in amusement—she could easily give her dress for the *première* as a token of her gratitude, because what she really ought to be grateful for was not that she had protected her dress from the rain, but that she had attained a state of grace through me as it were. With ever mounting cynicism, I thought to myself: "Everyone gets the angel they deserve, and just look at the angel she got: here I am, out of pure curiosity, coveting a dress which I have never seen. Now let's see how her soul is going to conform to the idea of an angel who is interested in dresses." It struck me in my arrogance, that I had no desire to be assigned as an angel to the fervid stupidity of that woman.

To be frank, being an angel was beginning to weigh upon me. I am all too familiar with the ways of the world: they call me good-hearted, and at least for some time I am disturbed by my own malice. I also began to understand why angels get upset: they are at everybody's beck and call. This had never occurred to me before. Unless I happened to be an angel rather low down in the hierarchy of angels. Who knows, perhaps I was just a novice angel. The complacent happiness of that woman began to depress me: she had exploited me to the full. She had converted my indecisive nature into a definite profession, she had transformed my spontaneity into an obligation, she had enslaved me, I who was an angel. Who knows, however, if I had not been sent into the world just for that moment of usefulness. This then, was my true worth. In the taxi I was not a fallen angel: I was an angel who came to her senses. I came to my senses and showed my displeasure. Any more nonsense and I would tell that woman in open revolt whose guardian angel I was: do me the favour of getting out of this taxi at once! But I curbed my tongue and supported the weight of my wings which felt ever more contrite because of the woman's enormous parcel. As my protegée, she continued to say nice things about me, or rather, about my function. I fumed inwardly. The woman sensed this and fell silent as if confused. By the time we reached Viveiros de Castro there was mute hostility between us.

—Listen, I said to her abruptly, because my spontaneity is a double-edged knife even for others, the taxi will drop me first then take you on.

—But, she said in surprise, a note of indignation creeping into her voice, then I shall have to make an enormous detour and end up by being late! You, on the other hand, would only have the slightest detour if you were to drop me off first.

—Of course, I replied dryly. But I will not allow any detours.

—I'll pay the whole fare! she insulted me with the same money with which she would have remembered to reward me.

—I shall pay the whole fare, I insulted her in return.

Upon alighting from the taxi, like someone who asks for nothing, I took great care to leave my wings folded on the taxi seat. I alighted with that profound lack of finesse which has saved me from angelical abysses. Free of wings, with a great swish of my invisible tail and with the hauteur which I reserve for taxi-drivers, I swept through the imposing entrance of the Visconde de Pelotas apartment block as regal as a queen.

What Men Live By

🐚 LEO TOLSTOY

"We know that we have passed out of death unto life, because we love the brethren. He that loveth not abideth in death."—I *Epistle St. John* iii. 14.

"Whoso hath the world's goods, and beholdeth his brother in need, and shutteth up his compassion from him, how doth the love of God abide in him? My little children, let us not love in word, neither with the tongue; but in deed and truth."—iii. 17–18.

"Love is of God; and every one that loveth is begotten of God, and knoweth God. He that loveth not knoweth not God; for God is love."—iv. 7–8.

"No man hath beheld God at any time; if we love one another, God abideth in us."—iv. 12.

"God is love; and he that abideth in love abideth in God, and God abideth in him."—iv. 16.

"If a man say, I love God, and hateth his brother, he is a liar; for he that loveth not his brother whom he hath seen, how can he love God whom he hath not seen?"—iv. 20.

· I ·

A shoemaker named Simon, who had neither house nor land of his own, lived with his wife and children in a peasant's hut and earned his living by his work. Work was cheap but bread was dear, and what he earned he spent for food. The man and his wife had but one sheep-skin coat between them for winter wear, and even that was worn to tatters, and this was the second year he had been wanting to buy sheep-skins for a new coat. Before winter Simon saved up a little money: a three-rúble note lay hidden in his wife's box, and five rúbles and twenty kopéks* were owed him by customers in the village.

So one morning he prepared to go to the village to buy the sheep-skins. He put on over his shirt his wife's wadded nankeen jacket, and over that he put his own cloth coat. He took the three-rúble note in his pocket, cut himself a stick to serve as a staff, and started

*One hundred kopéks make a rúble.

off after breakfast. "I'll collect the five rúbles that are due to me," thought he, "add the three I have got, and that will be enough to buy sheep-skins for the winter coat."

He came to the village and called at a peasant's hut, but the man was not at home. The peasant's wife promised that the money should be paid next week, but she would not pay it herself. Then Simon called on another peasant, but this one swore he had no money, and would only pay twenty kopéks which he owed for a pair of boots Simon had mended. Simon then tried to buy the sheep-skins on credit, but the dealer would not trust him.

"Bring your money," said he, "then you may have your pick of the skins. We know what debt-collecting is like."

So all the business the shoemaker did was to get the twenty kopéks for boots he had mended, and to take a pair of felt boots a peasant gave him to sole with leather.

Simon felt downhearted. He spent the twenty kopéks on vódka, and started homewards without having bought any skins. In the morning he had felt the frost; but now, after drinking the vódka, he felt warm even without a sheep-skin coat. He trudged along, striking his stick on the frozen earth with one hand, swinging the felt boots with the other, and talking to himself.

"I'm quite warm," said he, "though I have no sheep-skin coat. I've had a drop and it runs through all my veins. I need no sheep-skins. I go along and don't worry about anything. That's the sort of man I am! What do I care? I can live without sheep-skins. I don't need them. My wife will fret, to be sure. And, true enough, it *is* a shame; one works all day long and then does not get paid. Stop a bit! If you don't bring that money along, sure enough I'll skin you, blessed if

I don't. How's that? He pays twenty kopéks at a time! What can I do with twenty kopéks? Drink it—that's all one can do! Hard up, he says he is! So he may be—but what about me? You have house, and cattle, and everything; I've only what I stand up in! You have corn of your own growing, I have to buy every grain. Do what I will, I must spend three rúbles every week for bread alone. I come home and find the bread all used up and I have to fork out another rúble and a half. So just you pay up what you owe, and no nonsense about it!"

By this time he had nearly reached the shrine at the bend of the road. Looking up, he saw something whitish behind the shrine. The daylight was fading, and the shoemaker peered at the thing without being able to make out what it was. "There was no white stone here before. Can it be an ox? It's not like an ox. It has a head like a man, but it's too white; and what could a man be doing there?"

He came closer, so that it was clearly visible. To his surprise it really was a man, alive or dead, sitting naked, leaning motionless against the shrine. Terror seized the shoemaker, and he thought, "Some one has killed him, stripped him, and left him here. If I meddle I shall surely get into trouble."

So the shoemaker went on. He passed in front of the shrine so that he could not see the man. When he had gone some way he looked back, and saw that the man was no longer leaning against the shrine, but was moving as if looking towards him. The shoemaker felt more frightened than before, and thought, "Shall I go back to him or shall I go on? If I go near him something dreadful may happen. Who knows who the fellow is? He has not come here for any good. If I go near him he may jump up and throttle me, and there will be no getting away. Or if not, he'd still be a burden on one's hands. What could I do with a naked man? I couldn't give him my last clothes. Heaven only help me to get away!"

So the shoemaker hurried on, leaving the shrine behind him—when suddenly his conscience smote him and he stopped in the road.

"What are you doing, Simon?" said he to himself. "The man may be dying of want, and you slip past afraid. Have you grown so rich as to be afraid of robbers? Ah, Simon, shame on you!"

So he turned back and went up to the man.

· II ·

Simon approached the stranger, looked at him, and saw that he was a young man, fit, with no bruises on his body, but evidently freezing and frightened, and he sat there leaning back without looking up at Simon, as if too faint to lift his eyes. Simon went close to him and then the man seemed to wake up. Turning his head, he opened his eyes and looked into Simon's face. That one look was enough to make Simon fond of the man. He threw the felt boots on the ground, undid his sash, laid it on the boots, and took off his cloth coat.

"It's not a time for talking," said he. "Come, put this coat on at once!" And Simon took the man by the elbows and helped him to rise. As he stood there, Simon saw that his body was clean and in good condition, his hands and feet shapely, and his face good and kind. He threw his coat over the man's shoulders, but the latter could not find the sleeves. Simon guided his arms into them, and drawing the coat well on, wrapped it closely about him, tying the sash round the man's waist.

Simon even took off his torn cap to put it on the man's head, but then his own head felt cold and he thought: "I'm quite bald, while he has long curly hair." So he put his cap on his own head again. "It will be better to give him something for his feet," thought he; and he made the man sit down and helped him to put on the felt boots, saying, "There, friend, now move about and warm yourself. Other matters can be settled later on. Can you walk?"

The man stood up and looked kindly at Simon, but could not say a word.

"Why don't you speak?" said Simon. "It's too cold to stay here, we must be getting home. There now, take my stick, and if you're feeling weak lean on that. Now step out!"

The man started walking and moved easily, not lagging behind.

As they went along, Simon asked him, "And where do you belong to?"

"I'm not from these parts."

"I thought as much. I know the folks hereabouts. But how did you come to be there by the shrine?"

"I cannot tell."

"Has some one been ill-treating you?"

"No one has ill-treated me. God has punished me."

"Of course God rules all. Still, you'll have to find food and shelter somewhere. Where do you want to go to?"

"It is all the same to me."

Simon was amazed. The man did not look like a rogue, and he spoke gently, but yet he gave no account of himself. Still Simon thought, "Who knows what may have happened?" And he said to the stranger: "Well then, come home with me and at least warm yourself awhile."

So Simon walked towards his home, and the stranger kept up with him, walking at his side. The wind had risen and Simon felt it cold under his shirt. He was getting over his tipsiness by now and began to feel the frost. He went along sniffling and wrapping his wife's coat round him, and he thought to himself: "There now—talk about sheep-skins! I went out for sheep-skins and come home without even a coat to my back, and what is more, I'm bringing a naked man along with me. Matrëna won't be pleased!" And when he thought of his wife he felt sad; but when he looked at the stranger and remembered how he had looked up at him at the shrine, his heart was glad.

· III ·

Simon's wife had everything ready early that day. She had cut wood, brought water, fed the children, eaten her own meal, and now she sat thinking. She wondered when she ought to make bread: now or to-morrow? There was still a large piece left.

"If Simon has had some dinner in town," thought she, "and does not eat much for supper, the bread will last out another day."

She weighed the piece of bread in her hand again and again, and thought: "I won't make any more to-day. We have only enough flour left to bake one batch. We can manage to make this last out till Friday."

So Matrëna put away the bread, and sat down at the table to patch her husband's shirt. While she worked she thought how her husband was buying skins for a winter coat.

"If only the dealer does not cheat him. My good man is much too simple; he cheats nobody, but any child can take him in. Eight rúbles is a lot of money—he should get a good coat at that price.

Not tanned skins, but still a proper winter coat. How difficult it was last winter to get on without a warm coat. I could neither get down to the river, nor go out anywhere. When he went out he put on all we had, and there was nothing left for me. He did not start very early to-day, but still it's time he was back. I only hope he has not gone on the spree!"

Hardly had Matrëna thought this than steps were heard on the threshold and some one entered. Matrëna stuck her needle into her work and went out into the passage. There she saw two men: Simon, and with him a man without a hat and wearing felt boots.

Matrëna noticed at once that her husband smelt of spirits. "There now, he has been drinking," thought she. And when she saw that he was coatless, had only her jacket on, brought no parcel, stood there silent, and seemed ashamed, her heart was ready to break with disappointment. "He has drunk the money," thought she, "and has been on the spree with some good-for-nothing fellow whom he has brought home with him."

Matrëna let them pass into the hut, followed them in, and saw that the stranger was a young, slight man, wearing her husband's coat. There was no shirt to be seen under it, and he had no hat. Having entered, he stood neither moving nor raising his eyes, and Matrëna thought: "He must be a bad man—he's afraid."

Matrëna frowned, and stood beside the stove looking to see what they would do.

Simon took off his cap and sat down on the bench as if things were all right.

"Come, Matrëna; if supper is ready, let us have some."

Matrëna muttered something to herself and did not move, but stayed where she was, by the stove. She looked first at the one and then at the other of them and only shook her head. Simon saw that his wife was annoyed, but tried to pass it off. Pretending not to notice anything, he took the stranger by the arm.

"Sit down, friend," said he, "and let us have some supper."

The stranger sat down on the bench.

"Haven't you cooked anything for us?" said Simon.

Matrëna's anger boiled over. "I've cooked, but not for you. It seems to me you have drunk your wits away. You went to buy a sheep-skin coat, but come home without so much as the coat you had on, and bring a naked vagabond home with you. I have no supper for drunkards like you."

"That's enough, Matrëna. Don't wag your tongue without reason! You had better ask what sort of man—"

"And you tell me what you've done with the money?"

Simon found the pocket of the jacket, drew out the three-rúble note, and unfolded it.

"Here is the money. Trífonov did not pay, but promises to pay soon."

Matrëna got still more angry; he had bought no sheep-skins, but had put his only coat on some naked fellow and had even brought him to their house.

She snatched up the note from the table, took it to put away in safety, and said: "I have no supper for you. We can't feed all the naked drunkards in the world."

"There now, Matrëna, hold your tongue a bit. First hear what a man has to say—!"

"Much wisdom I shall hear from a drunken fool. I was right in not wanting to marry you—a drunkard. The linen my mother gave me you drank; and now you've been to buy a coat—and have drunk it too!"

Simon tried to explain to his wife that he had only spent twenty kopéks; tried to tell how he had found the man—but Matrëna would not let him get a word in. She talked nineteen to the dozen, and dragged in things that had happened ten years before.

Matrëna talked and talked, and at last she flew at Simon and seized him by the sleeve.

"Give me my jacket. It is the only one I have, and you must needs take it from me and wear it yourself. Give it here, you mangy dog, and may the devil take you."

Simon began to pull off the jacket, and turned a sleeve of it inside out; Matrëna seized the jacket and it burst its seams. She snatched it up, threw it over her head and went to the door. She meant to go out, but stopped undecided—she wanted to work off her anger, but she also wanted to learn what sort of a man the stranger was.

· IV ·

Matrëna stopped and said: "If he were a good man he would not be naked. Why, he hasn't even a shirt on him. If he were all right, you would say where you came across the fellow."

"That's just what I am trying to tell you," said Simon. "As I came to the shrine I saw him sitting all naked and frozen. It isn't quite the weather to sit about naked! God sent me to him or he would have perished. What was I to do? How do we know what may have happened to him? So I took him, clothed him, and brought him along. Don't be so angry, Matrëna. It is a sin. Remember, we must all die one day."

Angry words rose to Matrëna's lips, but she looked at the stranger and was silent. He sat on the edge of the bench, motionless, his hands folded on his knees, his head drooping on his breast, his eyes closed, and his brows knit as if in pain. Matrëna was silent, and Simon said: "Matrëna, have you no love of God?"

Matrëna heard these words, and as she looked at the stranger, suddenly her heart softened towards him. She came back from the door, and going to the stove she got out the supper. Setting a cup on the table, she poured out some *kvas*.* Then she brought out the last piece of bread and set out a knife and spoons.

"Eat, if you want to," said she.

Simon drew the stranger to the table.

"Take your place, young man," said he.

Simon cut the bread, crumbled it into the broth, and they began to eat. Matrëna sat at the corner of the table, resting her head on her hand and looking at the stranger.

And Matrëna was touched with pity for the stranger and began to feel fond of him. And at once the stranger's face lit up; his brows were no longer bent, he raised his eyes and smiled at Matrëna.

When they had finished supper, the woman cleared away the things and began questioning the stranger. "Where are you from?" said she.

"I am not from these parts."

"But how did you come to be on the road?"

"I may not tell."

*A non-intoxicating drink usually made from rye-malt and rye-flour.

"Did some one rob you?"

"God punished me."

"And you were lying there naked?"

"Yes, naked and freezing. Simon saw me and had pity on me. He took off his coat, put it on me, and brought me here. And you have fed me, given me drink, and shown pity on me. God will reward you!"

Matrëna rose, took from the window Simon's old shirt she had been patching, and gave it to the stranger. She also brought out a pair of trousers for him.

"There," said she, "I see you have no shirt. Put this on, and lie down where you please, in the loft or on the stove."*

The stranger took off the coat, put on the shirt, and lay down in the loft. Matrëna put out the candle, took the coat, and climbed to where her husband lay on the stove.

Matrëna drew the skirts of the coat over her and lay down but could not sleep; she could not get the stranger out of her mind.

When she remembered that he had eaten their last piece of bread and that there was none for to-morrow, and thought of the shirt and trousers she had given away, she felt grieved; but when she remembered how he had smiled, her heart was glad.

Long did Matrëna lie awake, and she noticed that Simon also was awake—he drew the coat towards him.

"Simon!"

---

*The brick stove, including the oven, in a Russian peasant's hut is usually built so as to leave a flat top, large enough to lie on, for those who want to sleep in a warm place.

"Well?"

"You have had the last of the bread and I have not put any to rise. I don't know what we shall do to-morrow. Perhaps I can borrow some of neighbour Martha."

"If we're alive we shall find something to eat."

The woman lay still awhile, and then said, "He seems a good man, but why does he not tell us who he is?"

"I suppose he has his reasons."

"Simon!"

"Well?"

"We give; but why does nobody give us anything?"

Simon did not know what to say; so he only said, "Let us stop talking," and turned over and went to sleep.

· V ·

In the morning Simon awoke. The children were still asleep; his wife had gone to the neighbour's to borrow some bread. The stranger alone was sitting on the bench, dressed in the old shirt and trousers, and looking upwards. His face was brighter than it had been the day before.

Simon said to him, "Well, friend; the belly wants bread and the naked body clothes. One has to work for a living. What work do you know?"

"I do not know any."

This surprised Simon, but he said, "Men who want to learn can learn anything."

"Men work and I will work also."

"What is your name?"

"Michael."

"Well, Michael, if you don't wish to talk about yourself, that is your own affair; but you'll have to earn a living for yourself. If you will work as I tell you, I will give you food and shelter."

"May God reward you! I will learn. Show me what to do."

Simon took yarn, put it round his thumb and began to twist it.

"It is easy enough—see!"

Michael watched him, put some yarn round his own thumb in the same way, caught the knack, and twisted the yarn also.

Then Simon showed him how to wax the thread. This also Michael mastered. Next Simon showed him how to twist the bristle in, and how to sew, and this, too, Michael learned at once.

Whatever Simon showed him he understood at once, and after three days he worked as if he had sewn boots all his life. He worked without stopping and ate little. When work was over he sat silently, looking upwards. He hardly went into the street, spoke only when necessary, and neither joked nor laughed. They never saw him smile, except that first evening when Matrëna gave them supper.

· VI ·

Day by day and week by week the year went round. Michael lived and worked with Simon. His fame spread till people said that no one sewed boots so neatly and strongly as Simon's workman, Michael; from all the district round people came to Simon for their boots, and he began to be well off.

One winter day, as Simon and Michael sat working, a carriage on sledge-runners, with three horses and with bells, drove up to the hut. They looked out of the window; the carriage stopped at their door, a fine servant jumped down from the box and opened the door. A gentleman in a fur coat got out and walked up to Simon's hut. Up jumped Matrëna and opened the door wide. The gentleman stooped to enter the hut, and when he drew himself up again his head nearly reached the ceiling and he seemed quite to fill his end of the room.

Simon rose, bowed, and looked at the gentleman with astonishment. He had never seen any one like him. Simon himself was lean, Michael was thin, and Matrëna was dry as a bone, but this man was like some one from another world: red-faced, burly, with a neck like a bull's, and looking altogether as if he were cast in iron.

The gentleman puffed, threw off his fur coat, sat down on the bench, and said, "Which of you is the master bootmaker?"

"I am, your Excellency," said Simon, coming forward.

Then the gentleman shouted to his lad, "Hey, Fédka, bring the leather!"

The servant ran in, bringing a parcel. The gentleman took the parcel and put it on the table.

"Untie it," said he. The lad untied it.

The gentleman pointed to the leather.

"Look here, shoemaker," said he, "do you see this leather?"

"Yes, your honour."

"But do you know what sort of leather it is?"

Simon felt the leather and said, "It is good leather."

"Good, indeed! Why, you fool, you never saw such leather before in your life. It's German, and cost twenty rúbles."

Simon was frightened, and said, "Where should I ever see leather like that?"

"Just so! Now, can you make it into boots for me?"

"Yes, your Excellency, I can."

Then the gentleman shouted at him: "You *can*, can you? Well, remember whom you are to make them for, and what the leather is. You must make me boots that will wear for a year, neither losing shape nor coming unsewn. If you can do it, take the leather and cut it up; but if you can't, say so. I warn you now, if your boots come unsewn or lose shape within a year I will have you put in prison. If they don't burst or lose shape for a year, I will pay you ten rúbles for your work.'

Simon was frightened and did not know what to say. He glanced at Michael and, nudging him with his elbow, whispered: "Shall I take the work?"

Michael nodded his head as if to say, "Yes, take it."

Simon did as Michael advised and undertook to make boots that would not lose shape or split for a whole year.

Calling his servant, the gentleman told him to pull the boot off his left leg, which he stretched out.

"Take my measure!" said he.

Simon stitched a paper measure seventeen inches long, smoothed it out, knelt down, wiped his hands well on his apron so as not to soil the gentleman's sock, and began to measure. He measured the sole, and round the instep, and began to measure the calf of the leg, but the paper was too short. The calf of the leg was as thick as a beam.

"Mind you don't make it too tight in the leg."

Simon stitched on another strip of paper. The gentleman twitched his toes about in his sock looking round at those in the hut, and as he did so he noticed Michael.

"Whom have you there?" asked he.

"That is my workman. He will sew the boots."

"Mind," said the gentleman to Michael, "remember to make them so that they will last me a year."

Simon also looked at Michael, and saw that Michael was not looking at the gentleman, but was gazing into the corner behind the gentleman, as if he saw some one there. Michael looked and looked, and suddenly he smiled, and his face became brighter.

"What are you grinning at, you fool?" thundered the gentleman. "You had better look to it that the boots are ready in time."

"They shall be ready in good time," said Michael.

"Mind it is so," said the gentleman, and he put on his boots and his fur coat, wrapped the latter round him, and went to the door. But he forgot to stoop, and struck his head against the lintel.

He swore and rubbed his head. Then he took his seat in the carriage and drove away.

When he had gone, Simon said: "There's a figure of a man for you! You could not kill him with a mallet. He almost knocked out the lintel, but little harm it did him."

And Matrëna said: "Living as he does, how should he not grow strong? Death itself can't touch such a rock as that."

· VII ·

Then Simon said to Michael: "Well, we have taken the work, but we must see we don't get into trouble over it. The leather is dear, and the gentleman hot-tempered. We must make no mistakes. Come, your eye is truer and your hands have become nimbler than mine, so you take this measure and cut out the boots. I will finish off the sewing of the vamps."

Michael did as he was told. He took the leather, spread it out on the table, folded it in two, took a knife and began to cut out.

Matrëna came and watched him cutting, and was surprised to see how he was doing it. Matrëna was accustomed to seeing boots made, and she looked and saw that Michael was not cutting the leather for boots, but was cutting it round.

She wished to say something, but she thought to herself: "Perhaps I do not understand how gentlemen's boots should be made. I suppose Michael knows more about it—and I won't interfere."

When Michael had cut up the leather he took a thread and began to sew not with two ends, as boots are sewn, but with a single end, as for soft slippers.

Again Matrëna wondered, but again she did not interfere. Michael sewed on steadily till noon. Then Simon rose for dinner, looked around, and saw that Michael had made slippers out of the gentleman's leather.

"Ah!" groaned Simon, and he thought, "How is it that Michael, who has been with me a whole year and never made a mistake before, should do such a dreadful thing? The gentleman ordered high boots, welted, with whole fronts, and Michael has made soft slippers with single soles, and has wasted the leather. What am I to say to the gentleman? I can never replace leather such as this."

And he said to Michael, "What are you doing, friend? You have ruined me! You know the gentleman ordered high boots, but see what you have made!"

Hardly had he begun to rebuke Michael, when "rat-tat" went the iron ring that hung at the door. Some one was knocking. They looked out of the window; a man had come on horseback and was fastening his horse. They opened the door, and the servant who had been with the gentleman came in.

"Good day," said he.

"Good day," replied Simon. "What can we do for you?"

"My mistress has sent me about the boots."

"What about the boots?"

"Why, my master no longer needs them. He is dead.'

"Is it possible?"

"He did not live to get home after leaving you, but died in the carriage. When we reached home and the servants came to help him alight, he rolled over like a sack. He was dead already, and so stiff that he could hardly be got out of the carriage. My mistress sent me here, saying: 'Tell the bootmaker that the gentleman who ordered boots of him and left the leather for them no longer needs the boots, but that he must quickly make soft slippers for the corpse. Wait till they are ready and bring them back with you.' That is why I have come."

Michael gathered up the remnants of the leather; rolled them up, took the soft slippers he had made, slapped them together, wiped them down with his apron, and handed them and the roll of leather to the servant, who took them and said: "Good-bye, masters, and good day to you!"

· VIII ·

Another year passed, and another, and Michael was now living his sixth year with Simon. He lived as before. He went nowhere, only spoke when necessary, and had only smiled twice in all those years—once when Matrëna gave him food, and a second time when the gentleman was in their hut. Simon was more than pleased with his workman. He never now asked him where he came from, and only feared lest Michael should go away.

They were all at home one day. Matrëna was putting iron pots in the oven; the children were running along the benches and looking out of the window; Simon was sewing at one window and Michael was fastening on a heel at the other.

One of the boys ran along the bench to Michael, leant on his shoulder, and looked out of the window.

"Look, Uncle Michael! There is a lady with little girls! She seems to be coming here. And one of the girls is lame."

When the boy said that, Michael dropped his work, turned to the window, and looked out into the street.

Simon was surprised. Michael never used to look out into the street, but now he pressed against the window, staring at something. Simon also looked out and saw that a well-dressed woman was really coming to his hut, leading by the hand two little girls in fur coats and woollen shawls. The girls could hardly be told one from the other, except that one of them was crippled in her left leg and walked with a limp.

The woman stepped into the porch and entered the passage. Feeling about for the entrance she found the latch, which she lifted and opened the door. She let the two girls go in first, and followed them into the hut.

"Good day, good folk!"

"Pray come in," said Simon. "What can we do for you?"

The woman sat down by the table. The two little girls pressed close to her knees, afraid of the people in the hut.

"I want leather shoes made for these two little girls, for spring."

"We can do that. We never have made such small shoes, but we can make them; either welved or turnover shoes, linen-lined. My man, Michael, is a master at the work."

Simon glanced at Michael and saw that he had left his work and was sitting with his eyes fixed on the little girls. Simon was surprised. It was true the girls were pretty, with black eyes, plump, and rosy-cheeked, and they wore nice kerchiefs and fur coats, but still Simon could not understand why Michael should look at them like that—just as if he had known them before. He was puzzled, but went on talking with the woman and arranging the price. Having fixed it, he prepared the measure. The woman lifted the lame girl on to her lap and said: "Take two measures from this little girl. Make one shoe for the lame foot and three for the sound one. They both have the same-sized feet. They are twins."

Simon took the measure and, speaking of the lame girl, said: "How did it happen to her? She is such a pretty girl. Was she born so?"

"No, her mother crushed her leg."

Then Matrëna joined in. She wondered who this woman was and whose the children were, so she said: "Are not you their mother, then?"

"No, my good woman; I am neither their mother nor any relation to them. They were quite strangers to me, but I adopted them."

"They are not your children and yet you are so fond of them?"

"How can I help being fond of them? I fed them both at my own breasts. I had a child of my own, but God took him. I was not so fond of him as I now am of these."

"Then whose children are they?"

· IX ·

The woman, having begun talking, told them the whole story.

"It is about six years since their parents died, both in one week: their father was buried on the Tuesday, and their mother died on the Friday. These orphans were born three days after their father's death, and their mother did not live another day. My husband and I were then living as peasants in the village. We were neighbours of theirs, our yard being next to theirs. Their father was a lonely man, a wood-cutter in the forest. When felling trees one day they let one fall on him. It fell across his body and crushed his bowels out. They hardly got him home before his soul went to God; and that same week his wife gave birth to twins—these little girls. She was poor and alone; she had no one, young or old, with her. Alone she gave them birth, and alone she met her death.

"The next morning I went to see her, but when I entered the hut, she, poor thing, was already stark and cold. In dying she had rolled on to this child and crushed her leg. The village folk came to the hut, washed the body, laid her out, made a coffin, and buried her. They were good folk. The babies were left alone. What was to be done with them? I was the only woman there who had a baby at the time. I was nursing my first-born—eight weeks old. So I took them for a time. The peasants came together, and thought and thought what to do with them; and at last they said to me: 'For the present, Mary, you had better keep the girls, and later on we will arrange what to do for them.' So I nursed the sound one at my breast, but at first I did not feed this crippled one. I did not suppose she would live. But then I thought to myself, why should the poor innocent suffer? I pitied her and began to feed her. And so I fed my own boy and these two—the three of them—at my own breast. I was young and strong and had good food, and God gave me so much milk that at times it even overflowed. I used sometimes to feed two at a time, while the third was waiting. When one had had enough I nursed the third. And God so ordered it that these grew up, while my own was buried before he was two years old. And I had no more children, though we prospered. Now my husband is working for the corn merchant at the mill. The pay is good and we are well off. But I have no children of my own, and how lonely I should be without these little girls! How can I help loving them! They are the joy of my life!"

She pressed the lame little girl to her with one hand, while with the other she wiped the tears from her cheeks.

And Matrëna sighed, and said: "The proverb is true that says, 'One may live without father or mother, but one cannot live without God.'"

So they talked together, when suddenly the whole hut was lighted up as though by summer lightning from the corner where Michael sat. They all looked towards him and saw him sitting, his hands folded on his knees, gazing upwards and smiling.

• X •

The woman went away with the girls. Michael rose from the bench, put down his work, and took off his apron. Then, bowing low to Simon and his wife, he said: "Farewell, masters. God has forgiven me. I ask your forgiveness, too, for anything done amiss."

And they saw that a light shone from Michael. And Simon rose, bowed down to Michael, and said: "I see, Michael, that you are no common man, and I can neither keep you nor question you. Only tell me this: how is it that when I found you and brought you home, you were gloomy, and when my wife gave you food you smiled at her and became brighter? Then when the gentleman came to order the boots, you smiled again and became brighter still? And now, when this woman brought the little girls, you smiled a third time and have become as bright as day? Tell me, Michael, why does your face shine so, and why did you smile those three times?"

And Michael answered: "Light shines from me because I have been punished, but now God has pardoned me. And I smiled three times, because God sent me to learn three truths, and I have learnt them. One I learnt when your wife pitied me, and that is why I smiled the first time. The second I learnt when the rich man ordered the boots, and then I smiled again. And now, when I saw those little girls, I learnt the third and last truth, and I smiled the third time."

And Simon said, "Tell me, Michael, what did God punish you for? and what were the three truths? that I, too, may know them."

And Michael answered: "God punished me for disobeying Him. I was an angel in heaven and disobeyed God. God sent me to fetch a woman's soul. I flew to earth, and saw a sick woman lying alone who had just given birth to twin girls. They moved feebly at their mother's side but she could not lift them to her breast. When she saw me, she understood that God had sent me for her soul, and she wept and said: 'Angel of God! My husband has just been buried, killed by a falling tree. I have neither sister, nor aunt, nor mother: no one to care for my orphans. Do not take my soul! Let me nurse my babes, feed them, and set them on their feet before I die. Children cannot live without father or mother.' And I hearkened to her.

I placed one child at her breast and gave the other into her arms, and returned to the Lord in heaven. I flew to the Lord, and said: 'I could not take the soul of the mother. Her husband was killed by a tree; the woman has twins and prays that her soul may not be taken. She says: "Let me nurse and feed my children, and set them on their feet. Children cannot live without father or mother." I have not taken her soul.' And God said: 'Go—take the mother's soul, and learn three truths: Learn *What dwells in man*, *What is not given to man*, and *What men live by*. When thou hast learnt these things, thou shalt return to heaven.' So I flew again to earth and took the mother's soul. The babes dropped from her breasts. Her body rolled over on the bed and crushed one babe, twisting its leg. I rose above the village, wishing to take her soul to God, but a wind seized me and my wings drooped and dropped off. Her soul rose alone to God, while I fell to earth by the roadside."

· XI ·

And Simon and Matrëna understood who it was that had lived with them, and whom they had clothed and fed. And they wept with awe and with joy. And the angel said: "I was alone in the field, naked. I had never known human needs, cold and hunger, till I became a man. I was famished, frozen, and did not know what to do. I saw, near the field I was in, a shrine built for God, and I went to it hoping to find shelter. But the shrine was locked and I could not enter. So I sat down behind the shrine to shelter myself at least from the wind. Evening drew on, I was hungry, frozen, and in pain. Suddenly I heard a man coming along the road. He carried a pair of boots and was talking to himself. For the first time since I became a man I saw the mortal face of a man, and his face seemed terrible to me and I turned from it. And I heard the man talking to himself of how to cover his body from the cold in winter, and how to feed wife and children. And I thought: 'I am perishing of cold and hunger and here is a man thinking only of how to clothe himself and his wife, and how to get bread for themselves. He cannot help me. When the man saw me he frowned and became still more terrible, and passed me by on the other side. I despaired; but suddenly I heard him coming back. I looked up and did not recognize the same man: before, I had seen death in his face; but now he was alive and I recognized in him the presence of God. He came up to me, clothed me, took me with him, and brought me to his home. I entered the house; a woman came to meet us and began to speak. The woman was still more terrible than the man had been; the spirit of death came from her mouth; I could not breathe for the stench of death that spread around her. She wished to drive me out into the cold, and I knew that if she did so she would die. Suddenly her husband spoke to her of God, and the woman changed at once. And when she brought me food and looked at me, I glanced at her and saw that death no longer dwelt in her; she had become alive, and in her too I saw God.

"Then I remembered the first lesson God had set me: *'Learn what dwells in man.'* And I understood that in man dwells Love! I was glad that God had already begun to show me what He had promised, and I smiled for the first time. But I had not yet learnt all. I did not yet know *What is not given to man*, and *What men live by*.

"I lived with you and a year passed. A man came to order boots that should wear for a year without losing shape or cracking. I looked at him, and suddenly, behind his shoulder, I saw my comrade—the angel of death. None but me saw that angel; but I knew him, and knew that before the sun set he would take that rich man's soul. And I thought to myself, 'The man is making preparations for a year and does not know that he will die before evening.' And I remembered God's second saying, *'Learn what is not given to man.'*

"What dwells in man I already knew. Now I learnt what is not given him. It is not given to man to know his own needs. And I smiled for the second time. I was glad to have seen my comrade angel—glad also that God had revealed to me the second saying.

"But I still did not know all. I did not know *What men live by.* And I lived on, waiting till God should reveal to me the last lesson. In the sixth year came the girl-twins with the woman; and I recognized the girls and heard how they had been kept alive. Having heard the story, I thought, 'Their mother besought me for the children's sake, and I believed her when she said that children cannot live without father or mother; but a stranger has nursed them, and has brought them up.' And when the woman showed her love for the children that were not her own, and wept over them, I saw in her the living God, and understood *What men live by.* And I knew that God had revealed to me the last lesson, and had forgiven my sin. And then I smiled for the third time."

• XII •

And the angel's body was bared, and he was clothed in light so that eye could not look on him; and his voice grew louder, as though it came not from him but from heaven above. And the angel said:

"I have learnt that all men live not by care for themselves, but by love.

"It was not given to the mother to know what her children needed for their life. Nor was it given to the rich man to know what he himself needed. Nor is it given to any man to know whether, when evening comes, he will need boots for his body or slippers for his corpse.

"I remained alive when I was a man, not by care of myself but because love was present in a passer-by, and because he and his wife pitied and loved me. The orphans remained alive not because of their mother's care, but because there was love in the heart of a woman, a stranger to them, who pitied and loved them. And all men live not by the thought they spend on their own welfare, but because love exists in man.

"I knew before that God gave life to men and desires that they should live; now I understood more than that.

"I understood that God does not wish men to live apart, and therefore he does not reveal to them what each one needs for himself; but he wishes them to live united, and therefore reveals to each of them what is necessary for all.

"I have now understood that though it seems to men that they live by care for themselves, in truth it is love alone by which they live. He who has love, is in God, and God is in him, for God is love."

And the angel sang praise to God, so that the hut trembled at his voice. The roof opened, and a column of fire rose from earth to heaven. Simon and his wife and children fell to the ground. Wings appeared upon the angel's shoulders and he rose into the heavens.

And when Simon came to himself the hut stood as before, and there was no one in it but his own family.

The Angel

 JAMES WRIGHT

Last night, before I came to bear
The clean edge of my wing upon the boulder,
I walked about the town.
The people seemed at peace that he was dead;
A beggar carried water out of a door,
And young men gathered round the corner
To spell the night.

I walked, like a folded bird, about the towers
And sang softly to the blue levels of evening,
I slid down treeless, featherless, bemused:
At curious faces whispering round a fire
And sniffing chestnuts sugared by a woman;
At a vague child heaving a beetle over
In dust, to see it swimming on its back.

Under an arch I found a woman lean
Weeping for loneliness: away from her
A young man whistle toward the crowds;
Out of an open window pigeons flew

And a slow dove fluted for nothing—the girl
Blew to the air a melody lost on me.

Laid in a pile of stone, how could he weep
For that calm town?
Looped in a yoke of darkened garden,
He murmured blood out of his heart for love,
Hallowed a soldier, took the savage kiss
And gave it back a warm caress;

Yet no one changed.

Tossing aside the worry of the place,
As someone threw an apple core across
A wall I walked beside, I sought delight
Pebble by pebble, song by song, and light
By light, singly, among the river boats.
Down to the river at the end I came.

But then a girl appeared, to wash her hair.
Struck stupid by her face,
I stood there, sick to love her, sick of sky.
The child, the beetle, chestnut fires, the song
Of girl and dove
Shuddered along my wings and arms.
She slipped her bodice off, and a last wave
Of shadow oiled her shoulder till it shone;
Lifting her arms to loosen the soft braids
She looked across the water. I looked down

And felt my wings waving aside the air,
Furious to fly. For I could never bear
Belly and breast and thigh against the ground.

Now, having heaved the hidden hollow open
As I was sent to do, seen Jesus waken
And guided the women there, I wait to rise.
To feel a weapon gouge between the ribs,
He hung with a shut mouth:
For curious faces round a chestnut fire,
For the slow fluting doves
Lost on a trellis, for the laughing girl
Who frightened me away.

But now I fumble at the single joy
Of dawn. On the pale ruffle of the lake
The ripples weave a color I can bear.
Under a hill I see the city sleep
And fade. The perfect pleasure of the eyes:
A tiny bird bathed in a bowl of air,
Carving a yellow ripple down the bines,
Posing no storm to blow my wings aside
As I drift upward dropping a white feather.

Angel Levine

❧ BERNARD MALAMUD

Manischevitz, a tailor, in his fifty-first year suffered many reverses and indignities. Previously a man of comfortable means, he overnight lost all he had, when his establishment caught fire and, after a metal container of cleaning fluid exploded, burned to the ground. Although Manischevitz was insured against fire, damage suits by two customers who had been hurt in the flames deprived him of every penny he had collected. At almost the same time, his son, of much promise, was killed in the war, and his daughter, without so much as a word of warning, married a lout and disappeared with him as off the face of the earth. Thereafter Manischevitz was victimized by excruciating backaches and found himself unable to work even as a presser—the only kind of work available to him—for more than an hour or two daily, because beyond that the pain from standing became maddening. His Fanny, a good wife and mother, who had taken in washing and sewing, began before his eyes to waste away. Suffering shortness of breath, she at last became seriously ill and took to her bed. The doctor, a former customer of Manischevitz, who out of pity treated them, at first had difficulty diagnosing her ailment but later put it down as hardening of the arteries at an advanced stage. He took Manischevitz aside, prescribed complete rest for her, and in whispers gave him to know there was little hope.

Throughout his trials Manischevitz had remained somewhat stoic, almost unbelieving that all this had descended upon his head, as if it were happening, let us say, to an acquaintance or some distant relative; it was in sheer quantity of woe incomprehensible. It was also ridiculous, unjust, and because he had always been a religious man, it was in a way an affront to God. Manischevitz believed this in all his suffering. When his burden had grown too crushingly heavy to be borne he prayed in his chair with shut hollow eyes: "My Dear God, sweetheart, did I deserve that this should happen to me?" Then recognizing the worthlessness of it, he put aside the complaint and prayed humbly for assistance: "Give Fanny back her health, and to me for myself that I shouldn't feel pain in every step. Help now or tomorrow is too late. This I don't have to tell you." And Manischevitz wept.

• • •

Manischevitz's flat, which he had moved into after the disastrous fire, was a meager one, furnished with a few sticks of chairs, a table, and bed, in one of the poorer sections of the city. There were three rooms: a small, poorly-papered living room; an apology for a kitchen, with a wooden icebox; and the comparatively large bedroom where Fanny lay in a sagging secondhand bed, gasping for breath. The bedroom was the warmest room of the house and it was here, after his outburst to God, that Manischevitz, by the light of two small bulbs overhead, sat reading his Jewish newspaper. He was not truly reading, because his thoughts were everywhere; however the print offered a convenient resting place for his eyes, and a word or two, when he permitted himself to comprehend them, had the momentary effect of helping him forget his troubles. After a short while he discovered, to his surprise, that he was actively scanning the news, searching for an item of great interest to him. Exactly what he thought he would read he couldn't say—until he realized, with some astonishment, that he was expecting to discover something about himself. Manischevitz put his paper down and looked up with the distinct impression that someone had entered the apartment, though he could not remember having heard the sound of the door opening. He looked around: the room was very still, Fanny sleeping, for once, quietly. Half-frightened, he watched her until he was satisfied she wasn't dead; then, still disturbed by the thought of an unannounced visitor, he stumbled into the living room and there had the shock of his life, for at the table sat a Negro reading a newspaper he had folded up to fit into one hand.

"What do you want here?" Manischevitz asked in fright.

The Negro put down the paper and glanced up with a gentle expression. "Good evening." He seemed not to be sure of himself, as if he had got into the wrong house. He was a large man, bonily built, with a heavy head covered by a hard derby, which he made no attempt to remove. His eyes seemed sad, but his lips, above which he wore a slight mustache, sought to smile; he was not otherwise prepossessing. The cuffs of his sleeves, Manischevitz noted, were frayed to the lining and the dark suit was badly fitted. He had very large feet. Recovering from his fright, Manischevitz guessed he had left the door open and was being visited by a case worker from the Welfare Department—some came at night—for he had recently applied for relief. Therefore he lowered himself into a chair opposite the Negro, trying, before the man's uncertain smile, to feel comfortable. The former tailor sat stiffly but patiently at the table, waiting for the investigator to take out his pad and pencil and begin asking questions; but before long he became convinced the man intended to do nothing of the sort.

"Who are you?" Manischevitz at last asked uneasily.

"If I may, insofar as one is able to, identify myself, I bear the name of Alexander Levine."

In spite of all his troubles Manischevitz felt a smile growing on his lips. "You said Levine?" he politely inquired.

The Negro nodded. "That is exactly right."

Carrying the jest farther, Manischevitz asked, "You are maybe Jewish?"

"All my life I was, willingly."

The tailor hesitated. He had heard of black Jews but had never met one. It gave an unusual sensation.

Recognizing in afterthought something odd about the tense of Levine's remark, he said doubtfully, "You ain't Jewish anymore?"

Levine at this point removed his hat, revealing a very white part in his black hair, but quickly replaced it. He replied, "I have recently been disincarnated into an angel. As such, I offer you my humble assistance, if to offer is within my province and ability—in the best sense." He lowered his eyes in apology. "Which calls for added explanation: I am what I am granted to be, and at present the completion is in the future."

"What kind of angel is this?" Manischevitz gravely asked.

"A bona fide angel of God, within prescribed limitations," answered Levine, "not to be confused with the members of any particular sect, order, or organization here on earth operating under a similar name."

Manischevitz was thoroughly disturbed. He had been expecting something but not this. What sort of mockery was it—provided Levine was an angel—of a faithful servant who had from childhood lived in the synagogues, always concerned with the word of God?

To test Levine he asked, "Then where are your wings?"

The Negro blushed as well as he was able. Manischevitz understood this from his changed expression. "Under certain circumstances we lose privileges and prerogatives upon returning to earth, no matter for what purpose, or endeavoring to assist whosoever."

"So tell me," Manischevitz said triumphantly, "how did you get here?"

"I was transmitted."

Still troubled, the tailor said, "If you are a Jew, say the blessing for bread."

Levine recited it in sonorous Hebrew.

Although moved by the familiar words Manischevitz still felt doubt that he was dealing with an angel.

"If you are an angel," he demanded somewhat angrily, "give me the proof."

Levine wet his lips. "Frankly, I cannot perform either miracles or near miracles, due to the fact that I am in a condition of probation. How long that will persist or even consist, I admit, depends on the outcome."

Manischevitz racked his brains for some means of causing Levine positively to reveal his true identity, when the Negro spoke again:

"It was given me to understand that both your wife and you require assistance of a salubrious nature?"

The tailor could not rid himself of the feeling that he was the butt of a jokester. Is this what a Jewish angel looks like? he asked himself. This I am not convinced.

He asked a last question. "So if God sends to me an angel, why a black? Why not a white that there are so many of them?"

"It was my turn to go next," Levine explained.

Manischevitz could not be persuaded. "I think you are a faker."

Levine slowly rose. His eyes showed disappointment and worry. "Mr. Manischevitz," he said tonelessly, "if you should desire me to be of assistance to you any time in the near future, or possibly before, I can be found"—he glanced at his fingernails—"in Harlem."

He was by then gone.

· · ·

The next day Manischevitz felt some relief from his backache and was able to work four hours at pressing. The day after, he put in six hours; and the third day four again. Fanny sat up a little and asked for some halvah to suck. But on the fourth day the stabbing, breaking ache afflicted his back, and Fanny again lay supine, breathing with blue-lipped difficulty.

Manischevitz was profoundly disappointed at the return of his active pain and suffering. He had hoped for a longer interval of easement, long enough to have some thought other than of himself and his troubles. Day by day, hour by hour, minute after minute, he lived in pain, pain his only memory, questioning the necessity of it, inveighing against it, also, though with affection, against God. Why *so much*, Gottenyu? If He wanted to teach His servant a lesson for some reason, some cause—the nature of His nature—to teach him, say, for reasons of his weakness, his pride, perhaps, during his years of prosperity, his frequent neglect of God—to give him a little lesson, why then any of the tragedies that had happened to him, any *one* would have sufficed to chasten him. But *all together*—the loss of both his children, his means of livelihood, Fanny's health and his— that was too much to ask one frail-boned man to endure. Who, after all, was Manischevitz that he had been given so much to suffer? A tailor. Certainly not a man of talent. Upon him suffering was largely wasted. It went nowhere, into nothing: into more suffering. His pain did not earn him bread, nor fill the cracks in the wall, nor lift, in the middle of the night, the kitchen table; only lay upon him, sleepless, so sharply oppressively that he could many times have cried out yet not heard himself through this thickness of misery.

In this mood he gave no thought to Mr. Alexander Levine, but at moments when the pain waivered, slightly diminishing, he sometimes wondered if he had been mistaken to dismiss him. A black Jew and angel to boot—very hard to believe, but suppose he *had* been sent to succor him, and he, Manischevitz, was in his blindness too blind to comprehend? It was this thought that put him on the knife-point of agony.

Therefore the tailor, after much self-questioning and continuing doubt, decided he would seek the self-styled angel in Harlem. Of course he had great difficulty, because he had not asked for specific directions, and movement was tedious to him. The subway took him to 116th Street, and from there he wandered in the dark world. It was vast and its lights lit nothing. Everywhere were shadows, often moving. Manischevitz hobbled along with the aid of a cane, and not knowing where to seek in the blackened tenement buildings, looked fruitlessly through store windows. In the stores he saw people and *everybody* was black. It was an amazing thing to observe.

When he was too tired, too unhappy to go farther, Manischevitz stopped in front of a tailor's store. Out of familiarity with the appearance of it, with some sadness he entered. The tailor, an old skinny Negro with a mop of woolly gray hair, was siting cross-legged on his workbench, sewing a pair of full-dress pants that had a razor slit all the way down the seat.

"You'll excuse me, please, gentleman," said Manischevitz, admiring the tailor's deft, thimbled fingerwork, "but you know maybe somebody by the name Alexander Levine?"

The tailor, who Manischevitz thought, seemed a little antagonistic to him, scratched his scalp.

"Cain't say I ever heared dat name."

"Alex-ander Lev-ine," Manischevitz repeated it.

The man shook his head. "Cain't say I heared."

About to depart, Manischevitz remembered to say: "He is an angel, maybe."

"Oh *him*," said the tailor clucking. "He hang out in dat honky tonk down here a ways." He pointed with his skinny finger and returned to the pants.

Manischevitz crossed the street against a red light and was almost run down by a taxi. On the block after the next, the sixth store from the corner was a cabaret, and the name in sparkling lights was Bella's. Ashamed to go in, Manischevitz gazed through the neon-lit window, and when the dancing couples had parted and drifted away, he discovered at a table on the side, towards the rear, Levine.

He was sitting alone, a cigarette butt hanging from the corner of his mouth, playing solitaire with a dirty pack of cards, and Manischevitz felt a touch of pity for him, for Levine had deteriorated in appearance. His derby was dented and had a gray smudge on the side. His ill-fitting suit was shabbier, as if he had been sleeping in it. His shoes and trouser cuffs were muddy, and his face was covered with an impenetrable stubble the color of licorice. Manischevitz, though deeply disappointed, was about to enter, when a big-breasted Negress in a purple evening gown appeared before Levine's table, and with much laughter through many white teeth, broke into a vigorous shimmy. Levine looked straight at Manischevitz with a haunted expression, but the tailor was too paralyzed to move or acknowledge it. As Bella's gyrations continued, Levine rose, his eyes lit in excitement. She embraced him with vigor, both his hands clasped around her big restless buttocks and they tangoed together across the floor, loudly applauded by the noisy customers. She seemed to have lifted Levine off his feet and his large shoes hung limp as they danced. They slid past the windows where Manischevitz, white-faced, stood staring in. Levine winked slyly and the tailor left for home.

.   .   .

Fanny lay at death's door. Through shrunken lips she muttered concerning her childhood, the sorrows of the marriage bed, the loss of her children, yet wept to live. Manischevitz tried not to listen, but even without ears he would have heard. It was not a gift. The doctor panted up the stairs, a broad but bland, unshaven man (it was Sunday) and soon shook his head. A day at most, or two. He left at once, not without pity, to spare himself Manischevitz's multiplied sorrow; the man who never stopped hurting. He would someday get him into a public home.

Manischevitz visited a synagogue and there spoke to God, but God had absented himself. The tailor searched his heart and found no hope. When she died he would live dead. He considered taking his life although he knew he wouldn't. Yet it was something to consider. Considering, you existed. He railed against God— Can you love a rock, a broom, an emptiness? Baring his chest, he smote the naked bones, cursing himself for having believed.

Asleep in a chair that afternoon, he dreamed of Levine. He was standing before a faded mirror, preening small decaying opalescent wings. "This means," mumbled Manischevitz, as he broke out of sleep, "that it is possible he could be an angel." Begging a neighbor lady to look in on Fanny and occasionally wet her lips with a few drops of water, he drew on his thin coat, gripped his walking stick, exchanged some pennies for a subway token, and rode to Harlem. He knew this act was the last desperate one of his woe: to go without belief, seeking a black magician to restore his wife to invalidism. Yet if there was no choice, he did at least what was chosen.

He hobbled to Bella's but the place had changed hands. It was now, as he breathed, a synagogue in a store. In the front, towards him, were several rows of empty wooden benches. In the rear stood the Ark, its portals of rough wood covered with rainbows of sequins; under it a long table on which lay the sacred scroll unrolled, illuminated by the dim light from a bulb on a chain overhead. Around the table, as if frozen to it and the scroll, which they all touched with their fingers, sat four Negroes wearing skullcaps. Now as they read the Holy Word, Manischevitz could, through the plate glass window, hear the singsong chant of their voices. One of them was old, with a gray beard. One was bubble-eyed. One was hump-backed. The fourth was a boy, no older than thirteen. Their heads moved in rhythmic swaying. Touched by this sight from his childhood and youth, Manischevitz entered and stood silent in the rear.

"Neshoma," said bubble eyes, pointing to the word with a stubby finger. "Now what dat mean?"

"That's the word that means soul," said the boy. He wore glasses.

"Let's git on wid de commentary," said the old man.

"Ain't necessary," said the humpback. "Souls is immaterial substance. That's all. The soul is derived in that manner. The immateriality is derived from the substance, and they both, causally an' otherwise, derived from the soul. There can be no higher."

"That's the highest."

"Over de top."

"Wait a minute," said bubble eyes. "I don't see what is dat immaterial substance. How come de one gits hitched up to de odder?" He addressed the humpback.

"Ask me something hard. Because it is substanceless immateriality. It couldn't be closer together, like all the parts of the body under one skin—closer."

"Hear now," said the old man.

"All you done is switched de words."

"It's the primum mobile, the substanceless substance from which comes all things that were incepted in the idea—you, me and everything and body else."

"Now how did all dat happen? Make it sound simple."

"It de speerit," said the old man. "On de face of de water moved de speerit. An' dat was good. It say so in de Book. From de speerit ariz de man."

"But now listen here. How come it become substance if it all de time a spirit?"

"God alone done dat."

"Holy! Holy! Praise His Name."

"But has dis spirit got some kind of a shade or color?" asked bubble eyes, deadpan.

"Man of course not. A spirit is a spirit."

"Then how come we is colored?" he said with a triumphant glare.

"Ain't got nothing to do wid dat."

"I still like to know."

"God put the spirit in all things," answered the boy. "He put it in the green leaves and the yellow flowers. He put it with the gold in the fishes and the blue in the sky. That's how come it came to us."

"Amen."

"Praise Lawd and utter loud His speechless name."

"Blow de bugle till it bust the sky."

They fell silent, intent upon the next word. Manischevitz approached them.

"You'll excuse me," he said. "I am looking for Alexander Levine. You know him maybe?"

"That's the angel," said the boy.

"Oh, *him*," snuffed bubble eyes.

"You'll find him at Bella's. It's the establishment right across the street," the humpback said.

Manischevitz said he was sorry that he could not stay, thanked them, and limped across the street. It was already night. The city was dark and he could barely find his way.

But Bella's was bursting with the blues. Through the window

Manischevitz recognized the dancing crowd and among them sought Levine. He was sitting loose-lipped at Bella's side table. They were tippling from an almost empty whiskey fifth. Levine had shed his old clothes, wore a shiny new checkered suit, pearl-gray derby, cigar, and big, two-tone button shoes. To the tailor's dismay, a drunken look had settled upon his formerly dignified face. He leaned towards Bella, tickled her ear lobe with his pinky, while whispering words that sent her into gales of raucous laughter. She fondled his knee.

Manischevitz, girding himself, pushed open the door and was not welcomed.

"This place reserved."

"Beat it, pale puss."

"Exit, Yankel, Semitic trash."

But he moved towards the table where Levine sat, the crowd breaking before him as he hobbled forward.

"Mr. Levine," he spoke in a trembly voice. "Is here Manischevitz."

Levine glared blearily. "Speak yo' piece, son."

Manischevitz shuddered. His back plagued him. Cold tremors tormented his crooked legs. He looked around, everybody was all ears.

"You'll excuse me. I would like to talk to you in a private place."

"Speak, Ah is a private pusson."

Bella laughed piercingly. "Stop it, boy, you killin' me."

Manischevitz, no end disturbed, considered fleeing but Levine addressed him:

"Kindly state the pu'pose of yo' communication with yo's truly."

The tailor wet cracked lips. "You are Jewish. This I am sure."

Levine rose, nostrils flaring. "Anythin' else yo' got to say?"

Manischevitz's tongue lay like stone.

"Speak now or fo'ever hold off."

Tears blinded the tailor's eyes. Was ever man so tried? Should he say he believed a half-drunken Negro to be an angel?

The silence slowly petrified.

Manischevitz was recalling scenes of his youth as a wheel in his mind whirred: believe, do not, yes, no, yes, no. The pointer pointed to yes, to between yes and no, to no, no it was yes. He sighed. It moved but one had still to make a choice.

"I think you are an angel from God." He said it in a broken voice, thinking, If you said it it was said. If you believed it you must say it. If you believed, you believed.

The hush broke. Everybody talked but the music began and they went on dancing. Bella, grown bored, picked up the cards and dealt herself a hand.

Levine burst into tears. "How you have humiliated me."

Manischevitz apologized.

"Wait'll I freshen up." Levine went to the men's room and returned in his old clothes.

No one said goodbye as they left.

They rode to the flat via subway. As they walked up the stairs Manischevitz pointed with his cane at his door.

"That's all been taken care of," Levine said. "You best go in while I take off."

Disappointed that it was so soon over but torn by curiosity, Manischevitz followed the angel up three flights to the roof. When he got there the door was already padlocked.

Luckily he could see through a small broken window. He heard an odd noise, as though of a whirring of wings, and when he strained for a wider view, could have sworn he saw a dark figure borne aloft on a pair of magnificent black wings.

A feather drifted down. Manischevitz gasped as it turned white, but it was only snowing.

He rushed downstairs. In the flat Fanny wielded a dust mop under the bed and then upon the cobwebs on the wall.

"A wonderful thing, Fanny," Manischevitz said. "Believe me, there are Jews everywhere."

A Crippled Angel

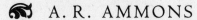 A. R. AMMONS

A crippled angel bent in a scythe of grief
mourned in an empty lot
    Passing by I stopped
amused that immortality should grieve
and said
It must be exquisite

Smoke came out of the angel's ears
        the axles
  of slow handwheels of grief
and under the white lids of its eyes

bulged tears of purple light
Watching the agony diffuse in
      shapeless loss
I interposed a harp
    The atmosphere possessed it eagerly
and the angel
saying prayers for the things of time

let its fingers drop and burn
the lyric strings provoking wonder

Grief sounded like an ocean rose
      in bright clothes
and the fire
breaking out on the limbs rising
caught up the branching wings
    in a flurry of ascent
Taking a bow I shot transfixing
the angel midair
              all miracle hanging fire
               on rafters of the sky

A Very Old Man with Enormous Wings

A TALE FOR CHILDREN

GABRIEL GARCÍA MÁRQUEZ

On the third day of rain they had killed so many crabs inside the house that Pelayo had to cross his drenched courtyard and throw them into the sea, because the newborn child had a temperature all night and they thought it was due to the stench. The world had been sad since Tuesday. Sea and sky were a single ash-gray thing and the sands of the beach, which on March nights glimmered like powdered light, had become a stew of mud and rotten shellfish. The light was so weak at noon that when Pelayo was coming back to the house after throwing away the crabs, it was hard for him to see what it was that was moving and groaning in the rear of the courtyard. He had to go very close to see that it was an old man, a very old man, lying face down in the mud, who, in spite of his tremendous efforts, couldn't get up, impeded by his enormous wings.

Frightened by that nightmare, Pelayo ran to get Elisenda, his wife, who was putting compresses on the sick child, and he took her to the rear of the courtyard. They both looked at the fallen body with mute stupor. He was dressed like a ragpicker. There were only a few faded hairs left on his bald skull and very few teeth in his mouth, and his pitiful condition of a drenched great-grandfather had taken away any sense of grandeur he might have had. His huge buzzard wings, dirty and half-plucked, were forever entangled in the mud. They looked at him so long and so closely that Pelayo and

Elisenda very soon overcame their surprise and in the end found him familiar. Then they dared speak to him, and he answered in an incomprehensible dialect with a strong sailor's voice. That was how they skipped over the inconvenience of the wings and quite intelligently concluded that he was a lonely castaway from some foreign ship wrecked by the storm. And yet, they called in a neighbor woman who knew everything about life and death to see him, and all she needed was one look to show them their mistake.

"He's an angel," she told them. "He must have been coming for the child, but the poor fellow is so old that the rain knocked him down."

On the following day everyone knew that a flesh-and-blood angel was held captive in Pelayo's house. Against the judgment of the wise neighbor woman, for whom angels in those times were the fugitive survivors of a celestial conspiracy, they did not have the heart to club him to death. Pelayo watched over him all afternoon from the kitchen, armed with his bailiff's club, and before going to bed he dragged him out of the mud and locked him up with the hens in the wire chicken coop. In the middle of the night, when the rain stopped, Pelayo and Elisenda were still killing crabs. A short time afterward the child woke up without a fever and with a desire to eat. Then they felt magnanimous and decided to put the angel on a raft with fresh water and provisions for three days and leave him to his fate on the high seas. But when they went out into the courtyard with the first light of dawn, they found the whole neighborhood in front of the chicken coop having fun with the angel, without the slightest reverence, tossing him things to eat through the openings in the wire as if he weren't a supernatural creature but a circus animal.

Father Gonzaga arrived before seven o'clock, alarmed at the strange news. By that time onlookers less frivolous than those at dawn had already arrived and they were making all kinds of conjectures concerning the captive's future. The simplest among them thought that he should be named mayor of the world. Others of sterner mind felt that he should be promoted to the rank of five-star general in order to win all wars. Some visionaries hoped that he could be put to stud in order to implant on earth a race of winged wise men who could take charge of the universe. But Father Gonzaga, before becoming a priest, had been a robust woodcutter. Standing by the wire, he reviewed his catechism in an instant and asked them to open the door so that he could take a close look at that pitiful man who looked more like a huge decrepit hen among the fascinated chickens. He was lying in a corner drying his open wings in the sunlight among the fruit peels and breakfast leftovers that the early risers had thrown him. Alien to the impertinences of the world, he only lifted his antiquarian eyes and murmured something in his dialect when Father Gonzaga went into the chicken coop and said good morning to him in Latin. The parish priest had his first suspicion of an imposter when he saw that he did not understand the language of God or know how to greet His ministers. Then he noticed that seen close up he was much too human: he had an unbearable smell of the outdoors, the back side of his wings was strewn with parasites and his main feathers had been mistreated by terrestrial winds, and nothing about him measured up to the proud dignity of angels. Then he came out of the chicken coop and in a brief sermon warned the curious against the risks of being ingenuous. He reminded them that the devil had the bad habit of making use of carnival tricks in order to confuse the unwary. He argued that if wings were not the essential element in determining the difference between a hawk and an airplane, they were even less so in the recognition of angels. Nevertheless, he promised to write a letter to his bishop so that the latter would write to his primate so that the latter would write to the Supreme Pontiff in order to get the final verdict from the highest courts.

His prudence fell on sterile hearts. The news of the captive angel spread with such rapidity that after a few hours the courtyard had the bustle of a marketplace and they had to call in troops with fixed bayonets to disperse the mob that was about to knock the house down. Elisenda, her spine all twisted from sweeping up so much marketplace trash, then got the idea of fencing in the yard and charging five cents admission to see the angel.

The curious came from far away. A traveling carnival arrived with a flying acrobat who buzzed over the crowd several times, but no one paid any attention to him because his wings were not those of an angel but, rather, those of a sidereal bat. The most unfortunate invalids on earth came in search of health: a poor woman who since childhood had been counting her heartbeats and had run out of numbers; a Portuguese man who couldn't sleep because the noise of the stars disturbed him; a sleepwalker who got up at night to undo the things he had done while awake; and many others with less serious ailments. In the midst of that shipwreck disorder that made the earth tremble, Pelayo and Elisenda were happy with fatigue, for in less than a week they had crammed their rooms with money and the line of pilgrims waiting their turn to enter still reached beyond the horizon.

The angel was the only one who took no part in his own act. He spent his time trying to get comfortable in his borrowed nest, befuddled by the hellish heat of the oil lamps and sacramental candles that had been placed along the wire. At first they tried to make him eat some mothballs, which, according to the wisdom of the wise neighbor woman, were the food prescribed for angels. But he turned them down, just as he turned down the papal lunches that the penitents brought him, and they never found out whether it was because he was an angel or because he was an old man that in the end he ate nothing but eggplant mush. His only supernatural virtue seemed to be patience. Especially during the first days, when the hens pecked at him, searching for the stellar parasites that proliferated in his wings, and the cripples pulled out feathers to touch their defective parts with, and even the most merciful threw stones at him, trying to get him to rise so they could see him standing. The only time they succeeded in arousing him was when they burned his side with an iron for branding steers, for he had been motionless for so many hours that they thought he was dead. He awoke with a start, ranting in his hermetic language and with tears in his eyes, and he flapped his wings a couple of times, which brought on a whirlwind of chicken dung and lunar dust and a gale of panic that did not seem to be of this world. Although many thought that his reaction had been one not of rage but of pain, from then on they were careful not to annoy him, because the majority understood that his passivity was not that of a hero taking his ease but that of a cataclysm in repose.

Father Gonzaga held back the crowd's frivolity with formulas of maidservant inspiration while awaiting the arrival of a final judgment on the nature of the captive. But the mail from Rome showed no sense of urgency. They spent their time finding out if the prisoner had a navel, if his dialect had any connection with Aramaic, how many times he could fit on the head of a pin, or whether he wasn't just a Norwegian with wings. Those meager letters might have come and gone until the end of time if a providential event had not put an end to the priest's tribulations.

It so happened that during those days, among so many other carnival attractions, there arrived in town the traveling show of the woman who had been changed into a spider for having disobeyed her parents. The admission to see her was not only less than the admission to see the angel, but people were permitted to ask her all manner of questions about her absurd state and to examine her up and down so that no one would ever doubt the truth of her horror. She was a frightful tarantula the size of a ram and with the head of a sad maiden. What was most heartrending, however, was not her outlandish shape but the sincere affliction with which she recounted the details of her misfortune. While still practically a child she had sneaked out of her parents' house to go to a dance, and while she was coming back through the woods after having danced all night without permission, a fearful thunderclap rent the sky in two and through the crack came the lightning bolt of brimstone that changed her into a spider. Her only nourishment came from the meatballs that charitable souls chose to toss into her mouth. A spectacle like that, full of so much human truth and with such a fearful lesson, was bound to defeat without even trying that of a haughty angel who scarcely deigned to look at mortals. Besides, the few miracles attributed to the angel showed a certain mental disorder, like the blind man who didn't recover his sight but grew three new teeth, or the paralytic who didn't get to walk but almost won the lottery, and the leper whose sores sprouted sunflowers. Those consolation miracles, which were more like mocking fun, had already ruined the angel's reputation when the woman who had been changed into a spider finally crushed him completely. That was how Father Gonzaga was cured forever of his insomnia and Pelayo's courtyard went back to being as empty as during the time it had rained for three days and crabs walked through the bedrooms.

The owners of the house had no reason to lament. With the money they saved they built a two-story mansion with balconies and gardens and high netting so that crabs wouldn't get in during the winter, and with iron bars on the windows so that angels wouldn't get in. Pelayo also set up a rabbit warren close to town and gave up his job as bailiff for good, and Elisenda bought some satin pumps with high heels and many dresses of iridescent silk, the kind worn on Sunday by the most desirable women in those times. The chicken coop was the only thing that didn't receive any attention. If they washed it down with creolin and burned tears of myrrh inside it every so often, it was not in homage to the angel but to drive away the dungheap stench that still hung everywhere like a ghost and was turning the new house into an old one. At first, when the child learned to walk, they were careful that he not get too close to the chicken coop. But then they began to lose their fears and got used to the smell, and before the child got his second teeth he'd gone inside the chicken coop to play, where the wires were falling apart. The angel was no less standoffish with him than with other mortals, but he tolerated the most ingenious infamies with the patience of a dog who had no illusions. They both came down with chicken pox at the same time. The doctor who took care of the child couldn't resist the temptation to listen to the angel's heart, and he found so much whistling in the heart and so many sounds in his kidneys that it seemed impossible for him to be alive. What surprised him most, however, was the logic of his wings. They seemed so natural on that completely human organism that he couldn't understand why other men didn't have them too.

When the child began school it had been some time since the sun and rain had caused the collapse of the chicken coop. The angel went dragging himself about here and there like a stray dying man. They would drive him out of the bedroom with a broom and a moment later find him in the kitchen. He seemed to be in so many places at the same time that they grew to think that he'd been duplicated, that he was reproducing himself all through the house, and the exasperated and unhinged Elisenda shouted that it was awful living in that hell full of angels. He could scarcely eat and his antiquarian eyes had also become so foggy that he went about bumping into posts. All he had left were the bare cannulae of his last feathers. Pelayo threw a blanket over him and extended him the charity of letting him sleep in the shed, and only then did they notice that he had a temperature at night, and was delirious with the tongue twisters of an old Norwegian. That was one of the few times they became alarmed, for they thought he was going to die and not even the wise neighbor woman had been able to tell them what to do with dead angels.

And yet he not only survived his worst winter, but seemed improved with the first sunny days. He remained motionless for several days in the farthest corner of the courtyard, where no one would see him, and at the beginning of December some large, stiff feathers began to grow on his wings, the feathers of a scarecrow, which looked more like another misfortune of decrepitude. But he must have known the reason for those changes, for he was quite careful that no one should notice them, that no one should hear the sea chanteys that he sometimes sang under the stars. One morning Elisenda was cutting some bunches of onions for lunch when a wind that seemed to come from the high seas blew into the kitchen. Then she went to the window and caught the angel in his first attempts at flight. They were so clumsy that his fingernails opened a furrow in the vegetable patch and he was on the point of knocking the shed down with the ungainly flapping that slipped on the light and couldn't get a grip on the air. But he did manage to gain altitude. Elisenda let out a sigh of relief, for herself and for him, when she saw him pass over the last houses, holding himself up in some way with the risky flapping of a senile vulture. She kept watching him even when she was through cutting the onions and she kept on watching until it was no longer possible for her to see him, because then he was no longer an annoyance in her life but an imaginary dot on the horizon of the sea.

PART FIVE

Angels in the Landscape

*A*ngels do not always make direct appearances. The world
may look bare of angels, and of God, too. Yet, in most of
the following poems and stories, even when the landscape seems
unoccupied by angels, their presence can be felt. They have
flown, subtly but unmistakably, into the very texture of ordinary
life, to inhabit the landscape and the kitchen, herons and rooks,
raspberries and whale sperm. They step effortlessly into our
language, and breathe at our elbows as we labor to write. Many
of these writings suggest a yearning for such angels, and such
inspiration. In various ways, these authors ask, How do we live in
a bare world? How do we survive the wait for angels? And how do
we discover the angelic presence when it arrives, whether in the
flash of a wing and the soaring of a poem, or in our
extraordinary selves?

Evening without Angels

❧ WALLACE STEVENS

*The great interests of man: air
and light, the joy of having a
body, the voluptuousness of
looking.*

MARIO ROSSI

Why seraphim like lutanists arranged
Above the trees? And why the poet as
Eternal *chef d'orchestre?*
      Air is air,
Its vacancy glitters round us everywhere.
Its sounds are not angelic syllables
But our unfashioned spirits realized
More sharply in more furious selves.

      And light
That fosters seraphim and is to them
Coiffeur of haloes, fecund jeweller—
Was the sun concoct for angels or for men?
Sad men made angels of the sun, and of
The moon they made their own attendant ghosts,
Which led them back to angels, after death.

Let this be clear that we are men of sun
And men of day and never of pointed night,
Men that repeat antiquest sounds of air
In an accord of repetitions. Yet,
If we repeat, it is because the wind
Encircling us, speaks always with our speech.

Light, too, encrusts us making visible
The motions of the mind and giving form
To moodiest nothings, as, desire for day
Accomplished in the immensely flashing East,
Desire for rest, in that descending sea
Of dark, which in its very darkening
Is rest and silence spreading into sleep.

... Evening, when the measure skips a beat
And then another, one by one, and all
To a seething minor swiftly modulate.
Bare night is best. Bare earth is best. Bare, bare,
Except for our own houses, huddled low
Beneath the arches and their spangled air,
Beneath the rhapsodies of fire and fire,
Where the voice that is in us makes a true response,
Where the voice that is great within us rises up,
As we stand gazing at the rounded moon.

Archangel

🐦 JOHN UPDIKE

Onyx and split cedar and bronze vessels lowered into still water: these things I offer. Porphyry, teakwood, jasmine, and myrrh: these gifts I bring. The sheen of my sandals is dulled by the dust of cloves. My wings are waxed with nectar. My eyes are diamonds in whose facets red gold is mirrored. My face is a mask of ivory: Love me. Listen to my promises:

Cold water will drip from the intricately chased designs of the bronze vessels. Thick-lipped urns will sweat in the fragrant cellars. The orchards never weary of bearing on my islands. The very leaves give nourishment. The banked branches never crowd the paths. The grape vines will grow unattended. The very seeds of the berries are sweet nuts. Why do you smile? Have you never been hungry?

The workmanship of the bowers will be immaculate. Where the elements are joined, the sword of the thinnest whisper will find its point excluded. Where the beams have been tapered, each swipe of the plane is continuous. Where the wood needed locking, pegs of a counter grain have been driven. The ceilings are high, for coolness, and the spaced shingles seal at the first breath of mist. Though the windows are open, the eaves of the roof are so wide that nothing of the rain comes into the rooms but its scent. Mats of perfect cleanness cover the floor. The fire is cupped in black rock and sustained on a smooth breast of ash. Have you never lacked shelter?

Where, then, has your life been touched? My pleasures are as specific as they are everlasting. The sliced edges of a fresh ream of laid paper, cream, stiff, rag-rich. The freckles of the closed eyelids of a woman attentive in the first white blush of morning. The ball diminishing well down the broad green throat of the first at Cape Ann. The good catch, a candy sun slatting the bleachers. The fair at the vanished poorhouse. The white arms of girls dancing, taffeta, white arms violet in the hollows music its ecstasies praise the white wrists of praise the white arms and the white paper trimmed the Euclidean proof of Pythagoras' theorem its tightening beauty the iridescence of an old copper found in the salt sand. The microscopic glitter in the ink of the letters of words that are your own. Certain moments, remembered or imagined, of childhood. Three-handed pinochle by the brown glow of the stained-glass lampshade, your parents out of their godliness silently wishing you to win. The Brancusi room, silent. *Pines and rocks*, by Cézanne; and *The Lace-Maker* in the Louvre hardly bigger than your spread hand.

Such glimmers I shall widen to rivers; nothing will be lost, not the least grain of remembered dust, and the multiplication shall be a thousand thousand fold; love me. Embrace me; come, touch my side, where honey flows. Do not be afraid. Why should my promises be vain? Jade and cinnamon: do you deny that such things exist? Why do you turn away? Is not my song a stream of balm? My arms are heaped with apples and ancient books; there is no harm in me; no. Stay. Praise me. Your praise of me is praise of yourself; wait. Listen. I will begin again.

Seascape

❧ ELIZABETH BISHOP

This celestial seascape, with white herons got up as angels,
flying as high as they want and as far as they want sidewise
in tiers and tiers of immaculate reflections;
the whole region, from the highest heron
down to the weightless mangrove island
with bright green leaves edged neatly with bird-droppings
like illumination in silver,
and down to the suggestively Gothic arches of the mangrove roots
and the beautiful pea-green back-pasture
where occasionally a fish jumps, like a wild-flower
in an ornamental spray of spray;
this cartoon by Raphael for a tapestry for a Pope:
it does look like heaven.
But a skeletal lighthouse standing there
in black and white clerical dress,
who lives on his nerves, thinks he knows better.
He thinks that hell rages below his iron feet,
that that is why the shallow water is so warm,
and he knows that heaven is not like this.
Heaven is not like flying or swimming,
but has something to do with blackness and a strong glare
and when it gets dark he will remember something
strongly worded to say on the subject.

A Still Moment

🐌 EUDORA WELTY

Lorenzo Dow rode the Old Natchez Trace at top speed upon a race horse, and the cry of the itinerant Man of God, "I must have souls! And souls I must have!" rang in his own windy ears. He rode as if never to stop, toward his night's appointment.

It was the hour of sunset. All the souls that he had saved and all those he had not took dusky shapes in the mist that hung between the high banks, and seemed by their great number and density to block his way, and showed no signs of melting or changing back into mist, so that he feared his passage was to be difficult forever. The poor souls that were not saved were darker and more pitiful than those that were, and still there was not any of the radiance he would have hoped to see in such a congregation.

"Light up, in God's name!" he called, in the pain of his disappointment.

Then a whole swarm of fireflies instantly flickered all around him, up and down, back and forth, first one golden light and then another, flashing without any of the weariness that had held back the souls. These were the signs sent from God that he had not seen the accumulated radiance of saved souls because he was not able, and that his eyes were more able to see the fire flies of the Lord than His blessed souls.

"Lord, give me the strength to see the angels when I am in Paradise," he said. "Do not let my eyes remain in this failing proportion to my loving heart always."

He gasped and held on. It was that day's complexity of horse-trading that had left him in the end with a Spanish race horse for which he was bound to send money in November from Georgia. Riding faster on the beast and still faster until he felt as if he were flying he sent thoughts of love with matching speed to his wife Peggy in Massachusetts. He found it effortless to love at a distance. He could look at the flowering trees and love Peggy in fullness, just as he could see his visions and love God. And Peggy, to whom he had not spoken until he could speak fateful words ("Would she accept of such an object as him?"), Peggy, the bride, with whom he had spent a few hours of time, showing of herself a small round handwriting, declared all in one letter, her first, that she felt the same as he, and that the fear was never of separation, but only of death.

Lorenzo well knew that it was Death that opened underfoot, that rippled by at night, that was the silence the birds did their singing in. He was close to death, closer than any animal or bird. On the back of one horse after another, winding them all, he was always riding toward it or away from it, and the Lord sent him directions with protection in His mind.

Just then he rode into a thicket of Indians taking aim with their new guns. One stepped out and took the horse by the bridle, it stopped at a touch, and the rest made a closing circle. The guns pointed.

"Incline!" The inner voice spoke sternly and with its customary lightning-quickness.

Lorenzo inclined all the way forward and put his head to the horse's silky mane, his body to its body, until a bullet meant for him would endanger the horse and make his death of no value. Prone he rode out through the circle of Indians, his obedience to the voice leaving him almost fearless, almost careless with joy.

But as he straightened and pressed ahead, care caught up with him again. Turning half-beast and half-divine, dividing himself like a heathen Centaur, he had escaped his death once more. But was it to be always by some metamorphosis of himself that he escaped, some humiliation of his faith, some admission to strength and argumentation and not frailty? Each time when he acted so it was at the command of an instinct that he took at once as the word of an angel, until too late, when he knew it was the word of the devil. He had roared like a tiger at Indians, he had submerged himself in water blowing the savage bubbles of the alligator, and they skirted him by. He had prostrated himself to appear dead, and deceived bears. But all the time God would have protected him in His own way, less hurried, more divine.

Even now he saw a serpent crossing the Trace, giving out knowing glances.

He cried, "I know you now!", and the serpent gave him one look out of which all the fire had been taken, and went away in two darts into the tangle.

He rode on, all expectation, and the voices in the throats of the wild beasts went, almost without his noticing when, into words. "Praise God," they said. "Deliver us from one another." Birds especially sang of divine love which was the one ceaseless protection. "Peace, in peace," were their words so many times when they spoke from the briars, in a courteous sort of inflection, and he turned his countenance toward all perched creatures with a benevolence striving to match their own.

He rode on past the little intersecting trails, letting himself be guided by voices and by lights. It was battlesounds he heard most, sending him on, but sometimes ocean sounds, that long beat of waves that would make his heart pound and retreat as heavily as they, and he despaired again in his failure in Ireland when he took a voyage and persuaded with the Catholics with his back against the door, and then ran away to their cries of "Mind the white hat!" But when he heard singing it was not the militant and sharp sound of Wesley's hymns, but a soft, tireless and tender air that had no beginning and no end, and the softness of distance, and he had pleaded with the Lord to find out if all this meant that it was wicked, but no answer had come.

Soon night would descend, and a camp-meeting ground ahead would fill with its sinners like the sky with its stars. How he hungered for them! He looked in prescience with a longing of love over the throng that waited while the flames of the torches threw change, change, change over their faces. How could he bring them enough, if it were not divine love and sufficient warning of all that could threaten them? He rode on faster. He was a filler of appointments, and he filled more and more, until his journeys up and down creation were nothing but a shuttle, driving back and forth upon the rich expanse of his vision. He was homeless by his own choice, he must be everywhere at some time, and somewhere soon. There hastening in the wilderness on his flying horse he gave the night's torch-lit crowd a premature benediction, he could not wait. He spread his arms out, one at a time for safety, and he wished, when they would all be gathered in by his tin horn blasts and the inspired words would go out over their heads, to brood above the entire and passionate life of the wide world, to become its rightful part.

He peered ahead. "Inhabitants of Time! The wilderness is your souls on earth!" he shouted ahead into the treetops. "Look about you, if you would view the conditions of your spirit, put here by the good Lord to show you and afright you. These wild places and these trails of awesome loneliness lie nowhere, nowhere, but in your heart."

. . .

A dark man, who was James Murrell the outlaw, rode his horse out of a cane brake and began going along beside Lorenzo without looking at him. He had the alternately proud and aggrieved look of a man believing himself to be an instrument in the hands of a power, and when he was young he said at once to strangers that he was being used by Evil, or sometimes he stopped a traveler by shouting, "Stop! I'm the Devil!" He rode along now talking and drawing out his talk, by some deep control of the voice gradually slowing the speed of Lorenzo's horse down until both the horses were softly trotting. He would have wondered that nothing he said was heard, not knowing that Lorenzo listened only to voices of whose heavenly origin he was more certain.

Murrell riding along with his victim-to-be, Murrell riding, was Murrell talking. He told away at his long tales, with always a distance and a long length of time flowing through them, and all centered about a silent man. In each the silent man would have done a piece of evil, a robbery or a murder, in a place of long ago, and it was all made for the revelation in the end that the silent man was Murrell himself, and the long story had happened yesterday, and the place *here*—the Natchez Trace. It would only take one dawning look for the victim to see that all of this was another story and he himself had listened his way into it, and that he too was about to recede in time (to where the dread was forgotten) for some listener and to live for a listener in the long ago. Destroy the present!—that must have been the first thing that was whispered in Murrell's heart—the living moment and the man that lives in it must die before you can go on. It was his habit to bring the journey—which might even take days—to a close with a kind of ceremony. Turning his face at last into the face of the victim, for he had never seen him before now, he would tower up with the sudden height of a man no longer the tale teller but the speechless protagonist, silent at last, one degree nearer the hero. Then he would murder the man.

But it would always start over. This man going forward was going backward with talk. He saw nothing, observed no world at all. The two ends of his journey pulled at him always and held him in a no-where, half asleep, smiling and witty, dangling his predicament. He was a murderer whose final stroke was over-long postponed, who had to bring himself through the greatest tedium to act, as if the whole wilderness, where he was born, were his impediment. But behind him and before him he kept in sight a victim, he saw a man fixed and stayed at the point of death—no matter how the man's eyes denied it, a victim, hands spreading to reach as if for the first time for life. Contempt! That is what Murrell gave that man.

Lorenzo might have understood, if he had not been in haste, that Murrell in laying hold of a man meant to solve his mystery of being. It was as if other men, all but himself, would lighten their hold on the secret, upon assault, and let it fly free at death. In his violence he was only treating of enigma. The violence shook his own body first, like a force gathering, and now he turned in the saddle.

Lorenzo's despair had to be kindled as well as his ecstasy, and could not come without that kindling. Before the awe-filled moment when the faces were turned up under the flares, as though an angel hand tipped their chins, he had no way of telling whether he would enter the sermon by sorrow or by joy. But at this moment the face of Murrell was turned toward him, turning at last, all solitary, in its full, and Lorenzo would have seized the man at once by his black coat and shaken him like prey for a lost soul, so instantly was he certain that the false fire was in his heart instead of the true fire. But Murrell, quick when he was quick, had put his own hand out, a restraining hand, and laid it on the wavelike flesh of the Spanish race horse, which quivered and shuddered at the touch.

They had come to a great live-oak tree at the edge of a low marsh-land. The burning sun hung low, like a head lowered on folded arms, and over the long reaches of violet trees the evening seemed still with thought. Lorenzo knew the place from having seen it among many in dreams, and he stopped readily and willingly. He drew rein, and Murrell drew rein, he dismounted and Murrell dismounted, he took a step, and Murrell was there too; and Lorenzo was not surprised at the closeness, how Murrell in his long dark coat and over it his dark face darkening still, stood beside him like a brother seeking light.

But in that moment instead of two men coming to stop by the great forked tree, there were three.

· · ·

From far away, a student, Audubon, had been approaching lightly on the wilderness floor, disturbing nothing in his lightness. The long day of beauty had led him this certain distance. A flock of purple finches that he tried for the first moment to count went over his head. He made a spelling of the soft *pet* of the ivory-billed woodpecker. He told himself always: remember.

Coming upon the Trace, he looked at the high cedars, azure and still as distant smoke overhead, with their silver roots trailing down on either side like the veins of deepness in this place, and he noted some fact to his memory—this earth that wears but will not crumble or slide or turn to dust, they say it exists in one other spot in the world, Egypt—and then forgot it. He walked quietly. All life used this Trace, and he liked to see the animals move along it in direct, oblivious journeys, for they had begun it and made it, the buffalo and deer and the small running creatures before man ever knew where he wanted to go, and birds flew a great mirrored course above. Walking beneath them Audubon remembered how in the cities he had seen these very birds in his imagination, calling them up whenever he wished, even in the hard and glittering outer parlors where if an artist were humble enough to wait, some idle hand held up promised money. He walked lightly and he went as carefully as he had started at two that morning, crayon and paper, a gun, and a small bottle of spirits disposed about his body. (*Note: "The mocking birds so gentle that they would scarcely move out of the way."*) He looked with care; great abundance had ceased to startle him, and he could see things one by one. In Natchez they had told him of many strange and marvelous birds that were to be found here. Their descriptions had been exact, complete, and wildly varying, and he took them for inventions and believed that like all the worldly things that came out of Natchez, they would be disposed of and shamed by any man's excursion into the reality of Nature.

In the valley he appeared under the tree, a sure man, very sure and tender, as if the touch of all the earth rubbed upon him and the stains of the flowery swamp had made him so.

Lorenzo welcomed him and turned fond eyes upon him. To

transmutate a man into an angel was the hope that drove him all over the world and never let him flinch from a meeting or withhold good-byes for long. This hope insistently divided his life into only two parts, journey and rest. There could be no night and day and love and despair and longing and satisfaction to make partitions in the single ecstasy of this alternation. All things were speech.

"God created the world," said Lorenzo, "and it exists to give testimony. Life is the tongue: speak."

But instead of speech there happened a moment of deepest silence.

Audubon said nothing because he had gone without speaking a word for days. He did not regard his thoughts for the birds and animals as susceptible, in their first change, to words. His long playing on the flute was not in its origin a talking to himself. Rather than speak to order or describe, he would always draw a deer with a stroke across it to communicate his need of venison to an Indian. He had only found words when he discovered that there is much otherwise lost that can be noted down each item in its own day, and he wrote often now in a journal, not wanting anything to be lost the way it had been, all the past, and he would write about a day, "Only sorry that the Sun Sets."

Murrell, his cheated hand hiding the gun, could only continue to smile at Lorenzo, but he remembered in malice that he had disguised himself once as an Evangelist, and his final words to this victim would have been, "One of my disguises was what you are."

Then in Murrell Audubon he saw what he thought of as "acquired sorrow"—that cumbrousness and darkness from which the naked Indian, coming just as he was made from God's hand, was so lightly free. He noted the eyes—the dark kind that loved to look through chinks, and saw neither closeness nor distance, light nor shade, wonder nor familiarity. They were narrowed to contract the heart, narrowed to make an averting plan. Audubon knew the finest-drawn tendons of the body and the working of their power, for he had touched them, and he supposed then that in man the enlargement of the eye to see started a motion in the hands to make or do, and that the narrowing of the eye stopped the hand and contracted the heart. Now Murrell's eyes followed an ant on a blade of grass, up the blade and down, many times in the single moment. Audubon had examined the Cave-In Rock where one robber had lived his hiding life, and the air in the cave was the cavelike air that enclosed this man, the same odor, flinty and dark. O secret life, he thought—is it true that the secret is withdrawn from the true disclosure, that man is a cave man, and that the openness I see, the ways through forests, the rivers brimming light, the wide arches where the birds fly, are dreams of freedom? If my origin is withheld from me, is my end to be unknown too? Is the radiance I see closed into an interval between two darks, or can it not illuminate them both and discover at last, though it cannot be spoken, what was thought hidden and lost?

In that quiet moment a solitary snowy heron flew down not far away and began to feed beside the marsh water.

At the single streak of flight, the ears of the race horse lifted, and the eyes of both horses filled with the soft lights of sunset, which in the next instant were reflected in the eyes of the men too as they all looked into the west toward the heron, and all eyes seemed infused with a sort of wildness.

Lorenzo gave the bird a triumphant look, such as a man may bestow upon his own vision, and thought, Nearness is near, lighted in a marsh-land, feeding at sunset. Praise God, His love has come visible.

Murrell, in suspicion pursuing all glances, blinking into a haze, saw only whiteness ensconced in darkness, as if it were a little luminous shell that drew in and held the eyesight. When he shaded his eyes, the brand "H.T." on his thumb thrust itself into his own vision, and he looked at the bird with the whole plan of the Mystic Rebellion darting from him as if in rays of the bright reflected light, and he stood looking proudly, leader as he was bound to become of the slaves, the brigands and outcasts of the entire Natchez country, with plans, dates, maps burning like a brand into his brain, and he saw himself proudly in a moment of prophecy going down rank after rank of successively bowing slaves to unroll and flaunt an awesome great picture of the Devil colored on a banner.

Audubon's eyes embraced the object in the distance and he could see it as carefully as if he held it in his hand. It was a snowy heron alone out of its flock. He watched it steadily, in his care noting the exact inevitable things. When it feeds it muddies the water with its foot. . . . It was as if each detail about the heron happened slowly in time, and only once. He felt again the old stab of wonder—what structure of life bridged the reptile's scale and the heron's feather? That knowledge too had been lost. He watched without moving. The bird was defenseless in the world except for the intensity of its life, and he wondered, how can heat of blood and speed of heart defend it? Then he thought, as always as if it were new and unbelievable, it has nothing in space or time to prevent its flight. And he waited, knowing that some birds will wait for a sense of their presence to travel to men before they will fly away from them.

Fixed in its pure white profile it stood in the precipitous moment, a plumicorn on its head, its breeding dress extended in rays, eating steadily the little water creatures. There was a little space between each man and the others, where they stood overwhelmed. No one could say the three had ever met, or that this moment of intersection had ever come in their lives, or its promise fulfilled. But before them the white heron rested in the grasses with the evening all around it, lighter and more serene than the evening, flight closed in its body, the circuit of its beauty closed, a bird seen and a bird still, its motion calm as if it were offered: Take my flight. . . .

What each of them had wanted was simply *all*. To save all souls, to destroy all men, to see and to record all life that filled this world—all, all—but now a single frail yearning seemed to go out of the three of them for a moment and to stretch toward this one snowy, shy bird in the marshes. It was as if three whirlwinds had drawn together at some center, to find there feeding in peace a snowy heron. Its own slow spiral of flight could take it away in its own time, but for a little it held them still, it laid quiet over them, and they stood for a moment unburdened. . . .

Murrell wore no mask, for his face was that, a face that was aware while he was somnolent, a face that watched for him, and listened for him, alert and nearly brutal, the guard of a planner. He was quick without that he might be slow within, he staved off time, he wandered and plotted, and yet his whole desire mounted in him toward the end (was this the end—the sight of a bird feeding at dusk?), toward the instant of confession. His incessant deeds were thick in his heart now, and flinging himself to the ground he thought wearily, when all these trees are cut down, and the Trace lost, then my Conspiracy that is yet to spread itself will be disclosed, and all the stone-loaded bodies of murdered men will be pulled up, and all everywhere will know poor Murrell. His look pressed upon Lorenzo, who stared upward, and Audubon, who was taking out his gun, and his eyes squinted up to them in pleading, as if to say, "How soon may I speak, and how soon will you pity me?" Then he looked back to the bird, and he thought if it would look at him a dread penetration would fill and gratify his heart.

Audubon in each act of life was aware of the mysterious origin he half-concealed and half-sought for. People along the way asked him in their kindness or their rudeness if it were true, that he was born a prince, and was the Lost Dauphin, and some said it was his secret, and some said that that was what he wished to find out before he died. But if it was his identity that he wished to discover, or if it was what a man had to seize beyond that, the way for him was by endless examination, by the care for every bird that flew in his path and every serpent that shone underfoot. Not one was enough; he looked deeper and deeper, on and on, as if for a particular beast or some legendary bird. Some men's eyes persisted in looking outward when they opened to look inward, and to their delight, there outflung was the astonishing world under the sky. When a man at last brought himself to face some mirror-surface he still saw the world looking back at him, and if he continued to look, to look closer and closer, what then? The gaze that looks outward must be trained without rest, to be indomitable. It must see as slowly as Murrell's ant in the grass, as exhaustively as Lorenzo's angel of God, and then, Audubon dreamed, with his mind going to his pointed brush, it must see like this, and he tightened his hand on the trigger of the gun and pulled it, and his eyes went closed. In memory the heron was all its solitude, its total beauty. All its whiteness could be seen from all sides at once, its pure feathers were as if counted and known and their array one upon the other would never be lost. But it was not from that memory that he could paint.

His opening eyes met Lorenzo's, close and flashing, and it was on seeing horror deep in them, like fires in abysses, that he recognized it for the first time. He had never seen horror in its purity and clarity until now, in bright blue eyes. He went and picked up the bird. He had thought it to be a female, just as one sees the moon as female; and so it was. He put it in his bag, and started away. But Lorenzo had already gone on, leaning a-tilt on the horse which went slowly.

Murrell was left behind, but he was proud of the dispersal, as if he had done it, as if he had always known that three men in simply being together and doing a thing can, by their obstinancy, take the pride out of one another. Each must go away alone, each send the others away alone. He himself had purposely kept to the wildest country in the world, and would have sought it out, the loneliest road. He looked about with satisfaction, and hid. Travelers were forever innocent, he believed: that was his faith. He lay in wait; his faith was in innocence and his knowledge was of ruin; and had these things been shaken? Now, what could possibly be outside his grasp? Churning all about him like a cloud about the sun was the great folding descent of his thought. Plans of deeds made his thoughts, and they rolled and mingled about his ears as if he heard a dark voice that rose up to overcome the wilderness voice, or was one with it. The night would soon come; and he had gone through the day.

Audubon, splattered and wet, turned back into the wilderness with the heron warm under his hand, his head still light in a kind of trance. It was undeniable, on some Sunday mornings, when he turned over and over his drawings they seemed beautiful to him, through what was dramatic in the conflict of life, or what was exact. What he would draw, and what he had seen, became for a moment one to him then. Yet soon enough, and it seemed to come in that same moment, like Lorenzo's horror and the gun's firing, he knew that even the sight of the heron which surely he alone had appreciated, had not been all his belonging, and that never could any vision, even any simple sight, belong to him or to any man. He knew that the best he could make would be, after it was apart from his hand, a dead thing and not a live thing, never the essence, only a sum of parts; and that it would always meet with a stranger's sight, and never be one with the beauty in any other man's head in the world. As he had seen the bird most purely at its moment of death, in some fatal way, in his care for looking outward, he saw his long labor most revealingly at the point where it met its limit. Still carefully, for he was trained to see well in the dark, he walked on into the deeper woods, noting all sights, all sounds, and was gentler than they as he went.

In the woods that echoed yet in his ears, Lorenzo riding slowly looked back. The hair rose on his head and his hands began to shake with cold, and suddenly it seemed to him that God Himself, just now, thought of the Idea of Separateness. For surely He had never thought of it before, when the little white heron was flying down to feed. He could understand God's giving Separateness first and then giving Love to follow and heal in its wonder; but God had reversed this, and given Love first and then Separateness, as though it did not matter to Him which came first. Perhaps it was that God never counted the moments of Time; Lorenzo did that, among his tasks of love. Time did not occur to God. Therefore—did He even know of it? How to explain Time and Separateness back to God, Who had never thought of them, Who could let the whole world come to grief in a scattering moment?

Lorenzo brought his cold hands together in a clasp and stared through the distance at the place where the bird had been as if he saw it still; as if nothing could really take away what had happened to him, the beautiful little vision of the feeding bird. Its beauty had been greater than he could account for. The sweat of rapture poured down from his forehead, and then he shouted into the marshes.

"Tempter!"

He whirled forward in the saddle and began to hurry the horse to its high speed. His camp ground was far away still, though even now they must be lighting the torches and gathering in the multitudes, so that at the appointed time he would duly appear in their midst, to deliver his address on the subject of "In that day when all hearts shall be disclosed."

Then the sun dropped below the trees, and the new moon, slender and white, hung shyly in the west.

Monday or Tuesday

 VIRGINIA WOOLF

Lazy and indifferent, shaking space easily from his wings, knowing his way, the heron passes over the church beneath the sky. White and distant, absorbed in itself, endlessly the sky covers and uncovers, moves and remains. A lake? Blot the shores of it out! A mountain? Oh, perfect—the sun gold on its slopes. Down that falls. Ferns then, or white feathers, for ever and ever—

Desiring truth, awaiting it, laboriously distilling a few words, for ever desiring—(a cry starts to the left, another to the right. Wheels strike divergently. Omnibuses conglomerate in conflict)—for ever desiring—(the clock asseverates with twelve distinct strokes that it is midday; light sheds gold scales; children swarm)—for ever desiring truth. Red is the dome; coins hang on the trees; smoke trails from the chimneys; bark, shout, cry "Iron for sale"—and truth?

Radiating to a point men's feet and women's feet, black or gold-encrusted—(This foggy weather—Sugar? No, thank you—The commonwealth of the future)—the firelight darting and making the room red, save for the black figures and their bright eyes, while outside a van discharges, Miss Thingummy drinks tea at her desk, and plate-glass preserves fur coats—

Flaunted, leaf-light, drifting at corners, blown across the wheels, silver-splashed, home or not home, gathered, scattered, squandered in separate scales, swept up, down, torn, sunk, assembled—and truth?

Now to recollect by the fireside on the white square of marble. From ivory depths words rising shed their blackness, blossom and penetrate. Fallen the book; in the flame, in the smoke, in the momentary sparks—or now voyaging, the marble square pendant, minarets beneath and the Indian seas, while space rushes blue and stars glint—truth? or now, content with closeness?

Lazy and indifferent the heron returns; the sky veils her stars; then bares them.

Herring Gulls: First Winter

LESLIE ELLEN MOORE

To Harriet

The old man said that gulls
soar for the joy of it
learn their resurrection in the pines
looming, skimming in and out
of crimson, threading
yes, he said
and all we know
are darker shadows on the sea
a swerve to blue
unravelling to blue
while mottled spans of brown on brown
design their heaven
dream magenta
yes, he said
and pull their glowing wings into the weft
beyond the sea, deep in the pines
emerging seraphim

From *Moby Dick*

❧ HERMAN MELVILLE

That whale of Stubb's so dearly purchased, was duly brought to the Pequod's side, where all those cutting and hoisting operations previously detailed, were regularly gone through, even to the baling of the Heidelburgh Tun, or Case.

While some were occupied with this latter duty, others were employed in dragging away the larger tubs, so soon as filled with the sperm; and when the proper time arrived, this same sperm was carefully manipulated ere going to the try-works, of which anon.

It had cooled and crystallized to such a degree, that when, with several others, I sat down before a large Constantine's bath of it, I found it strangely concreted into lumps, here and there rolling about in the liquid part. It was our business to squeeze these lumps back into fluid. A sweet and unctuous duty! No wonder that in old times this sperm was such a favorite cosmetic. Such a clearer! such a sweetener! such a softener! such a delicious mollifier! After having my hands in it for only a few minutes, my fingers felt like eels, and began, as it were, to serpentine and spiralize.

As I sat there at my ease, cross-legged on the deck; after the bitter exertion at the windlass; under a blue tranquil sky; the ship under indolent sail, and gliding so serenely along; as I bathed my hands among those soft, gentle globules of infiltrated tissues, woven almost within the hour; as they richly broke to my fingers, and discharged all their opulence, like fully ripe grapes their wine; as I snuffed up that uncontaminated aroma,—literally and truly, like the smell of spring violets; I declare to you, that for the time I lived as in a musky meadow; I forgot all about our horrible oath; in that inexpressible sperm, I washed my hands and my heart of it; I almost began to credit the old Paracelsan superstition that sperm is of rare virtue in allaying the heat of anger: while bathing in that bath, I felt divinely free from all ill-will, or petulence, or malice, of any sort whatsoever.

Squeeze! squeeze! squeeze! all the morning long; I squeezed that sperm till I myself almost melted into it; I squeezed that sperm till a strange sort of insanity came over me; and I found myself unwittingly squeezing my co-laborers' hands in it, mistaking their hands for the gentle globules. Such an abounding, affectionate, friendly, loving feeling did this avocation beget; that at last I was continually squeezing their hands, and looking up into their eyes sentimentally; as much as to say,—Oh! my dear fellow beings, why should we longer cherish any social acerbities, or know the slightest ill-humor or envy! Come; let us squeeze hands all round; nay, let us all squeeze ourselves into each other; let us squeeze ourselves universally into the very milk and sperm of kindness.

Would that I could keep squeezing that sperm for ever! For now, since by many prolonged, repeated experiences, I have perceived that in all cases man must eventually lower, or at least shift, his conceit of attainable felicity; not placing it anywhere in the intellect or the fancy; but in the wife, the heart, the bed, the table, the saddle, the fire-side, the country; now that I have perceived all this, I am ready to squeeze case eternally. In thoughts of the visions of the night, I saw long rows of angels in paradise, each with his hands in a jar of spermaceti.

Angel of Blizzards and Blackouts

ANNE SEXTON

Angel of blizzards and blackouts, do you know raspberries,
those rubies that sat in the green of my grandfather's garden?
You of the snow tires, you of the sugary wings, you freeze
me out. Let me crawl through the patch. Let me be ten.
Let me pick those sweet kisses, thief that I was,
as the sea on my left slapped its applause.

Only my grandfather was allowed there. Or the maid
who came with a scullery pan to pick for breakfast.
She of the rolls that floated in the air, she of the inlaid
woodwork all greasy with lemon, she of the feather and dust,
not I. Nonetheless I came sneaking across the salt lawn
in bare feet and jumping-jack pajamas in the spongy dawn.

Oh Angel of the blizzard and blackout, Madam white face,
take me back to that red mouth, that July 21st place.

Black Rook in Rainy Weather

SYLVIA PLATH

On the stiff twig up there
Hunches a wet black rook
Arranging and rearranging its feathers in the rain.
I do not expect a miracle
Or an accident

To set the sight on fire
In my eye, nor seek
Any more in the desultory weather some design,
But let spotted leaves fall as they fall,
Without ceremony, or portent.

Although, I admit, I desire,
Occasionally, some backtalk
From the mute sky, I can't honestly complain:
A certain minor light may still
Lean incandescent

Out of kitchen table or chair
As if a celestial burning took
Possession of the most obtuse objects now and then—
Thus hallowing an interval
Otherwise inconsequent

By bestowing largesse, honor,
One might say love. At any rate, I now walk
Wary (for it could happen
Even in this dull, ruinous landscape); skeptical,
Yet politic; ignorant

Of whatever angel may choose to flare
Suddenly at my elbow. I only know that a rook
Ordering its black feathers can so shine
As to seize my senses, haul
My eyelids up, and grant

A brief respite from fear
Of total neutrality. With luck,
Trekking stubborn through this season
Of fatigue, I shall
Patch together a content

Of sorts. Miracles occur,
If you care to call those spasmodic
Tricks of radiance miracles. The wait's begun again,
The long wait for the angel,
For that rare, random descent.

Revelation

 FLANNERY O'CONNOR

The doctor's waiting room, which was very small, was almost full when the Turpins entered and Mrs. Turpin, who was very large, made it look even smaller by her presence. She stood looming at the head of the magazine table set in the center of it, a living demonstration that the room was inadequate and ridiculous. Her little bright black eyes took in all the patients as she sized up the seating situation. There was one vacant chair and a place on the sofa occupied by a blond child in a dirty blue romper who should have been told to move over and make room for the lady. He was five or six, but Mrs. Turpin saw at once that no one was going to tell him to move over. He was slumped down in the seat, his arms idle at his sides and his eyes idle in his head; his nose ran unchecked.

Mrs. Turpin put a firm hand on Claud's shoulder and said in a voice that included anyone who wanted to listen, "Claud, you sit in that chair there," and gave him a push down into the vacant one. Claud was florid and bald and sturdy, somewhat shorter than Mrs. Turpin, but he sat down as if he were accustomed to doing what she told him to.

Mrs. Turpin remained standing. The only man in the room besides Claud was a lean stringy old fellow with a rusty hand spread out on each knee, whose eyes were closed as if he were asleep or dead or pretending to be so as not to get up and offer her his seat. Her gaze settled agreeably on a well-dressed gray-haired lady whose eyes met hers and whose expression said: if that child belonged to me, he would have some manners and move over—there's plenty of room there for you and him too.

Claud looked up with a sigh and made as if to rise.

"Sit down," Mrs. Turpin said. "You know you're not supposed to stand on that leg. He has an ulcer on his leg," she explained.

Claud lifted his foot onto the magazine table and rolled his trouser leg up to reveal a purple swelling on a plump marble-white calf.

"My!" the pleasant lady said. "How did you do that?"

"A cow kicked him," Mrs. Turpin said.

"Goodness!" said the lady.

Claud rolled his trouser leg down.

"Maybe the little boy would move over," the lady suggested, but the child did not stir.

"Somebody will be leaving in a minute," Mrs. Turpin said. She could not understand why a doctor—with as much money as they made charging five dollars a day to just stick their head in the hospital door and look at you—couldn't afford a decent-sized waiting room. This one was hardly bigger than a garage. The table was cluttered with limp-looking magazines and at one end of it there was a big green glass ash tray full of cigarette butts and cotton wads with little blood spots on them. If she had had anything to do with the running of the place, that would have been emptied every so often. There were no chairs against the wall at the head of the room. It had a rectangular-shaped panel in it that permitted a view of the office where the nurse came and went and the secretary listened to the radio. A plastic fern in a gold pot sat in the opening and trailed its fronds down almost to the floor. The radio was softly playing gospel music.

Just then the inner door opened and a nurse with the highest stack of yellow hair Mrs. Turpin had ever seen put her face in the crack and called for the next patient. The woman sitting beside Claud grasped the two arms of her chair and hoisted herself up; she pulled her dress free from her legs and lumbered through the door where the nurse had disappeared.

Mrs. Turpin eased into the vacant chair, which held her tight as a corset. "I wish I could reduce," she said, and rolled her eyes and gave a comic sigh.

"Oh, *you* aren't fat," the stylish lady said.

"Ooooo I am too," Mrs. Turpin said. "Claud he eats all he wants to and never weighs over one hundred and seventy-five pounds, but me I just look at something good to eat and I gain some weight," and her stomach and shoulders shook with laughter. "You can eat all you want to, can't you, Claud?" she asked, turning to him.

Claud only grinned.

"Well, as long as you have such a good disposition," the stylish lady said, "I don't think it makes a bit of difference what size you are. You just can't beat a good disposition."

Next to her was a fat girl of eighteen or nineteen, scowling into a thick blue book which Mrs. Turpin saw was entitled *Human Development*. The girl raised her head and directed her scowl at Mrs. Turpin as if she did not like her looks. She appeared annoyed that anyone should speak while she tried to read. The poor girl's face was blue with acne and Mrs. Turpin thought how pitiful it was to have a face like that at that age. She gave the girl a friendly smile but the girl only scowled the harder. Mrs. Turpin herself was fat but she had always had good skin, and, though she was forty-seven years old, there was not a wrinkle in her face except around her eyes from laughing too much.

Next to the ugly girl was the child, still in exactly the same position, and next to him was a thin leathery old woman in a cotton print dress. She and Claud had three sacks of chicken feed in their pump house that was in the same print. She had seen from the first that the child belonged with the old woman. She could tell by the way they sat—kind of vacant and white-trashy, as if they would sit there until Doomsday if nobody called and told them to get up. And at right angles but next to the well-dressed pleasant lady was a lank-faced woman who was certainly the child's mother. She had on a yellow sweat shirt and wine-colored slacks, both gritty-looking, and the rims of her lips were stained with snuff. Her dirty yellow hair was tied behind with a little piece of red paper ribbon. Worse than niggers any day, Mrs. Turpin thought.

The gospel hymn playing was, "When I looked up and He looked down," and Mrs. Turpin, who knew it, supplied the last line mentally, "And wona these days I know I'll we-eara crown."

Without appearing to, Mrs. Turpin always noticed people's feet. The well-dressed lady had on red and gray suede shoes to match her dress. Mrs. Turpin had on her good black patent leather pumps. The ugly girl had on Girl Scout shoes and heavy socks. The old woman had on tennis shoes and the white-trashy mother had on what appeared to be bedroom slippers, black straw with gold braid threaded through them—exactly what you would have expected her to have on.

Sometimes at night when she couldn't go to sleep, Mrs. Turpin would occupy herself with the question of who she would have chosen to be if she couldn't have been herself. If Jesus had said to her before he made her, "There's only two places available for you.

You can either be a nigger or white-trash," what would she have said? "Please, Jesus, please," she would have said, "just let me wait until there's another place available," and he would have said, "No, you have to go right now and I have only those two places so make up your mind." She would have wiggled and squirmed and begged and pleaded but it would have been no use and finally she would have said, "All right, make me a nigger then—but that don't mean a trashy one." And he would have made her a neat clean respectable Negro woman, herself but black.

Next to the child's mother was a red-headed youngish woman, reading one of the magazines and working a piece of chewing gum, hell for leather, as Claud would say. Mrs. Turpin could not see the woman's feet. She was not white-trash, just common. Sometimes Mrs. Turpin occupied herself at night naming the classes of people. On the bottom of the heap were most colored people, not the kind she would have been if she had been one, but most of them; then next to them—not above, just away from—were the white-trash; then above them were the home-owners, and above them the home-and-land owners, to which she and Claud belonged. Above she and Claud were people with a lot of money and much bigger houses and much more land. But here the complexity of it would begin to bear in on her, for some of the people with a lot of money were common and ought to be below she and Claud and some of the people who had good blood had lost their money and had to rent and then there were colored people who owned their homes and land as well. There was a colored dentist in town who had two red Lincolns and a swimming pool and a farm with registered white-face cattle on it. Usually by the time she had fallen asleep all the classes of people were moiling and roiling around in her head, and she would dream they were all crammed in together in a box car, being ridden off to be put in a gas oven.

"That's a beautiful clock," she said and nodded to her right. It was a big wall clock, the face encased in a brass sunburst.

"Yes, it's very pretty," the stylish lady said agreeably. "And right on the dot too," she added, glancing at her watch.

The ugly girl beside her cast an eye upward at the clock, smirked, then looked directly at Mrs. Turpin and smirked again. Then she returned her eyes to her book. She was obviously the lady's daughter because, although they didn't look anything alike as to disposition, they both had the same shape of face and the same blue eyes. On the lady they sparkled pleasantly but in the girl's seared face they appeared alternately to smolder and to blaze.

What if Jesus had said, "All right, you can be white-trash or a nigger or ugly"!

Mrs. Turpin felt an awful pity for the girl, though she thought it was one thing to be ugly and another to act ugly.

The woman with the snuff-stained lips turned around in her chair and looked up at the clock. Then she turned back and appeared to look a little to the side of Mrs. Turpin. There was a cast in one of her eyes. "You want to know wher you can get you one of themther clocks?" she asked in a loud voice.

"No, I already have a nice clock," Mrs. Turpin said. Once somebody like her got a leg in the conversation, she would be all over it.

"You can get you one with green stamps," the woman said. "That's most likely wher he got hisn. Save you up enough, you can get you most anythang. I got me some joo'ry."

Ought to have got you a wash rag and some soap, Mrs. Turpin thought.

"I get contour sheets with mine," the pleasant lady said.

The daughter slammed her book shut. She looked straight in front of her, directly through Mrs. Turpin and on through the yellow curtain and the plate glass window which made the wall behind her. The girl's eyes seemed lit all of a sudden with a peculiar light, an unnatural light like night road signs give. Mrs. Turpin turned her head to see if there was anything going on outside that she should see, but she could not see anything. Figures passing cast only a pale shadow through the curtain. There was no reason the girl should single her out for her ugly looks.

"Miss Finley," the nurse said, cracking the door. The gum-chewing woman got up and passed in front of her and Claud and went into the office. She had on red high-heeled shoes.

Directly across the table, the ugly girl's eyes were fixed on Mrs. Turpin as if she had some very special reason for disliking her.

"This is wonderful weather, isn't it?" the girl's mother said.

"It's good weather for cotton if you can get the niggers to pick it," Mrs. Turpin said, "but niggers don't want to pick cotton any more. You can't get the white folks to pick it and now you can't get the niggers—because they got to be right up there with the white folks."

"They gonna *try* anyways," the white-trash woman said, leaning forward.

"Do you have one of the cotton-picking machines?" the pleasant lady asked.

"No," Mrs. Turpin said, "they leave half the cotton in the field. We don't have much cotton anyway. If you want to make it farming now, you have to have a little of everything. We got a couple of acres of cotton and a few hogs and chickens and just enough white-face that Claud can look after them himself."

"One thang I don't want," the white-trash woman said, wiping her mouth with the back of her hand. "Hogs. Nasty stinking things, a-gruntin and a-rootin all over the place."

Mrs. Turpin gave her the merest edge of her attention. "Our hogs are not dirty and they don't stink," she said. "They're cleaner than some children I've seen. Their feet never touch the ground. We have a pig-parlor—that's where you raise them on concrete," she explained to the pleasant lady, "and Claud scoots them down with the hose every afternoon and washes off the floor." Cleaner by far than that child right there, she thought. Poor nasty little thing. He had not moved except to put the thumb of his dirty hand into his mouth.

The woman turned her face away from Mrs. Turpin. "I know I wouldn't scoot down no hog with no hose," she said to the wall.

You wouldn't have no hog to scoot down, Mrs. Turpin said to herself.

"A-gruntin and a-rootin and a-groanin," the woman muttered.

"We got a little of everything," Mrs. Turpin said to the pleasant lady. "It's no use in having more than you can handle yourself with help like it is. We found enough niggers to pick our cotton this year but Claud he has to go after them and take them home again in the evening. They can't walk that half a mile. No they can't. I tell you," she said and laughed merrily, "I sure am tired of buttering up niggers, but you got to love em if you want em to work for you. When they come in the morning, I run out and I say, 'Hi yawl this morning?' and when Claud drives them off to the field I just wave to beat the band and they just wave back." And she waved her hand rapidly to illustrate.

"Like you read out of the same book," the lady said, showing she understood perfectly.

"Child, yes," Mrs. Turpin said. "And when they come in from the field, I run out with a bucket of icewater. That's the way it's going to be from now on," she said. "You may as well face it."

"One thang I know," the white-trash woman said. "Two thangs I ain't going to do: love no niggers or scoot down no hog with no hose." And she let out a bark of contempt.

The look that Mrs. Turpin and the pleasant lady exchanged indicated they both understood that you had to *have* certain things before you could *know* certain things. But every time Mrs. Turpin exchanged a look with the lady, she was aware that the ugly girl's peculiar eyes were still on her, and she had trouble bringing her attention back to the conversation.

"When you got something," she said, "you got to look after it." And when you ain't got a thing but breath and britches, she added to herself, you can afford to come to town every morning and just sit on the Court House coping and spit.

A grotesque revolving shadow passed across the curtain behind her and was thrown palely on the opposite wall. Then a bicycle clattered down against the outside of the building. The door opened and a colored boy glided in with a tray from the drugstore. It had two large red and white paper cups on it with tops on them. He was a tall, very black boy in discolored white pants and a green nylon shirt. He was chewing gum slowly, as if to music. He set the tray down in the office opening next to the fern and stuck his head through to look for the secretary. She was not in there. He rested his arms on the ledge and waited, his narrow bottom stuck out, swaying to the left and right. He raised a hand over his head and scratched the base of his skull.

"You see that button there, boy?" Mrs. Turpin said. "You can punch that and she'll come. She's probably in the back somewhere."

"Is that right?" the boy said agreeably, as if he had never seen the button before. He leaned to the right and put his finger on it. "She sometime out," he said and twisted around to face his audience, his elbows behind him on the counter. The nurse appeared and he twisted back again. She handed him a dollar and he rooted in his pocket and made the change and counted it out to her. She gave him fifteen cents for a tip and he went out with the empty tray. The heavy door swung to slowly and closed at length with the sound of suction. For a moment no one spoke.

"They ought to send all them niggers back to Africa," the white-trash woman said. "That's wher they come from in the first place."

"Oh, I couldn't do without my good colored friends," the pleasant lady said.

"There's a heap of things worse than a nigger," Mrs. Turpin agreed. "It's all kinds of them just like it's all kinds of us."

"Yes, and it takes all kinds to make the world go round," the lady said in her musical voice.

As she said it, the raw-complexioned girl snapped her teeth together. Her lower lip turned downwards and inside out, revealing the pale pink inside of her mouth. After a second it rolled back up. It was the ugliest face Mrs. Turpin had ever seen anyone make and for a moment she was certain that the girl had made it at her. She was looking at her as if she had known and disliked her all her life—all of Mrs. Turpin's life, it seemed too, not just all the girl's life. Why, girl, I don't even know you, Mrs. Turpin said silently.

She forced her attention back to the discussion. "It wouldn't be practical to send them back to Africa," she said. "They wouldn't want to go. They got it too good here."

"Wouldn't be what they wanted—if I had anythang to do with it," the woman said.

"It wouldn't be a way in the world you could get all the niggers back over there," Mrs. Turpin said. "They'd be hiding out and lying down and turning sick on you and wailing and hollering and raring and pitching. It wouldn't be a way in the world to get them over there."

"They got over here," the trashy woman said. "Get back like they got over."

"It wasn't so many of them then," Mrs. Turpin explained.

The woman looked at Mrs. Turpin as if here was an idiot indeed but Mrs. Turpin was not bothered by the look, considering where it came from.

"Nooo," she said, "they're going to stay here where they can go to New York and marry white folks and improve their color. That's what they all want to do, every one of them, improve their color."

"You know what comes of that, don't you?" Claud asked.

"No, Claud, what?" Mrs. Turpin said.

Claud's eyes twinkled. "White-faced niggers," he said with never a smile.

Everybody in the office laughed except the white-trash and the ugly girl. The girl gripped the book in her lap with white fingers. The trashy woman looked around her from face to face as if she thought they were all idiots. The old woman in the feed sack dress continued to gaze expressionless across the floor at the high-top shoes of the man opposite her, the one who had been pretending to be asleep when the Turpins came in. He was laughing heartily, his hands still spread out on his knees. The child had fallen to the side and was lying now almost face down in the old woman's lap.

While they recovered from their laughter, the nasal chorus on the radio kept the room from silence.

> *"You go to blank blank*
> *And I'll go to mine*
> *But we'll all blank along*
> *To-geth-ther,*
> *And all along the blank*
> *We'll hep eachother out*
> *Smile-ling in any kind of*
> *Weath-ther!"*

Mrs. Turpin didn't catch every word but she caught enough to agree with the spirit of the song and it turned her thoughts sober. To help anybody out that needed it was her philosophy of life. She never spared herself when she found somebody in need, whether they were white or black, trash or decent. And of all she had to be thankful for, she was most thankful that this was so. If Jesus had said, "You can be high society and have all the money you want and be thin and svelte-like, but you can't be a good woman with it," she would have had to say, "Well don't make me that then. Make me a good woman and it don't matter what else, how fat or how ugly or how poor!" Her heart rose. He had not made her a nigger or white-trash or ugly! He had made her herself and given her a little of everything. Jesus, thank you! she said. Thank you thank you thank you! Whenever she counted her blessings she felt as buoyant as if she weighed one hundred and twenty-five pounds instead of one hundred and eighty.

"What's wrong with your little boy?" the pleasant lady asked the white-trashy woman.

"He has a ulcer," the woman said proudly. "He ain't give me a minute's peace since he was born. Him and her are just alike," she said, nodding at the old woman, who was running her leathery fingers through the child's pale hair. "Look like I can't get nothing down them two but Co' Cola and candy."

That's all you try to get down em, Mrs. Turpin said to herself. Too lazy to light the fire. There was nothing you could tell her about people like them that she didn't know already. And it was not just that they didn't have anything. Because if you gave them everything, in two weeks it would all be broken or filthy or they would have chopped it up for lightwood. She knew all this from her own experience. Help them you must, but help them you couldn't.

All at once the ugly girl turned her lips inside out again. Her eyes fixed like two drills on Mrs. Turpin. This time there was no mistaking that there was something urgent behind them.

Girl, Mrs. Turpin exclaimed silently, I haven't done a thing to you! The girl might be confusing her with somebody else. There was no need to sit by and let herself be intimidated. "You must be in college," she said boldly, looking directly at the girl. "I see you reading a book there."

The girl continued to stare and pointedly did not answer.

Her mother blushed at this rudeness. "The lady asked you a question, Mary Grace," she said under her breath.

"I have ears," Mary Grace said.

The poor mother blushed again. "Mary Grace goes to Wellesley College," she explained. She twisted one of the buttons on her dress. "In Massachusetts," she added with a grimace. "And in the summer she just keeps right on studying. Just reads all the time, a real book worm. She's done real well at Wellesley; she's taking English and Math and History and Psychology and Social Studies," she rattled on, "and I think it's too much. I think she ought to get out and have fun."

The girl looked as if she would like to hurl them all through the plate glass window.

"Way up north," Mrs. Turpin murmured and thought, well, it hasn't done much for her manners.

"I'd almost rather to have him sick," the white-trash woman said, wrenching the attention back to herself. "He's so mean when he ain't. Look like some children just take natural to meanness. It's some gets bad when they get sick but he was the opposite. Took sick and turned good. He don't give me no trouble now. It's me waitin to see the doctor," she said.

If I was going to send anybody back to Africa, Mrs. Turpin thought, it would be your kind, woman. "Yes, indeed," she said aloud, but looking up at the ceiling, "it's a heap of things worse than a nigger." And dirtier than a hog, she added to herself.

"I think people with bad dispositions are more to be pitied than anyone on earth," the pleasant lady said in a voice that was decidedly thin.

"I thank the Lord he has blessed me with a good one," Mrs. Turpin said. "The day has never dawned that I couldn't find something to laugh at."

"Not since she married me anyways," Claud said with a comical straight face.

Everybody laughed except the girl and the white-trash.

Mrs. Turpin's stomach shook. "He's such a caution," she said, "that I can't help but laugh at him."

The girl made a loud ugly noise through her teeth.

Her mother's mouth grew thin and tight. "I think the worst thing in the world," she said, "is an ungrateful person. To have everything and not appreciate it. I know a girl," she said, "who has parents who would give her anything, a little brother who loves her dearly, who is getting a good education, who wears the best clothes, but who can never say a kind word to anyone, who never smiles, who just criticizes and complains all day long."

"Is she too old to paddle?" Claud asked.

The girl's face was almost purple.

"Yes," the lady said, "I'm afraid there's nothing to do but leave her to her folly. Some day she'll wake up and it'll be too late."

"It never hurt anyone to smile," Mrs. Turpin said. "It just makes you feel better all over."

"Of course," the lady said sadly, "but there are just some people you can't tell anything to. They can't take criticism."

"If it's one thing I am," Mrs. Turpin said with feeling, "it's grateful. When I think who all I could have been besides myself and what all I got, a little of everything, and a good disposition besides, I just feel like shouting, 'Thank you, Jesus, for making everything the way it is!' It could have been different!" For one thing, somebody else could have got Claud. At the thought of this, she was flooded with gratitude and a terrible pang of joy ran through her. "Oh thank you, Jesus, Jesus, thank you!" she cried aloud.

The book struck her directly over her left eye. It struck almost at the same instant that she realized the girl was about to hurl it. Before she could utter a sound, the raw face came crashing across the table toward her, howling. The girl's fingers sank like clamps into the soft flesh of her neck. She heard the mother cry out and Claud shout, "Whoa!" There was an instant when she was certain that she was about to be in an earthquake.

All at once her vision narrowed and she saw everything as if it were happening in a small room far away, or as if she were looking at it through the wrong end of a telescope. Claud's face crumpled and fell out of sight. The nurse ran in, then out, then in again. Then the gangling figure of the doctor rushed out of the inner door. Magazines flew this way and that as the table turned over. The girl fell with a thud and Mrs. Turpin's vision suddenly reversed itself and she saw everything large instead of small. The eyes of the white-trashy woman were staring hugely at the floor. There the girl, held down on one side by the nurse and on the other by her mother, was wrenching and turning in their grasp. The doctor was kneeling astride her, trying to hold her arm down. He managed after a second to sink a long needle into it.

Mrs. Turpin felt entirely hollow except for her heart which swung from side to side as if it were agitated in a great empty drum of flesh.

"Somebody that's not busy call for the ambulance," the doctor said in the off-hand voice young doctors adopt for terrible occasions.

Mrs. Turpin could not have moved a finger. The old man who had been sitting next to her skipped nimbly into the office and made the call, for the secretary still seemed to be gone.

"Claud!" Mrs. Turpin called.

He was not in his chair. She knew she must jump up and find him but she felt like some one trying to catch a train in a dream, when everything moves in slow motion and the faster you try to run the slower you go.

"Here I am," a suffocated voice, very unlike Claud's, said.

He was doubled up in the corner on the floor, pale as paper, holding his leg. She wanted to get up and go to him but she could not move. Instead, her gaze was drawn slowly downward to the churning face on the floor, which she could see over the doctor's shoulder.

The girl's eyes stopped rolling and focused on her. They seemed a much lighter blue than before, as if a door that had been tightly closed behind them was now open to admit light and air.

Mrs. Turpin's head cleared and her power of motion returned. She leaned forward until she was looking directly into the fierce brilliant eyes. There was no doubt in her mind that the girl did know her, knew her in some intense and personal way, beyond time and place and condition. "What you got to say to me?" she asked hoarsely and held her breath, waiting, as for a revelation.

The girl raised her head. Her gaze locked with Mrs. Turpin's. "Go back to hell where you came from, you old wart hog," she whispered. Her voice was low but clear. Her eyes burned for a moment as if she saw with pleasure that her message had struck its target.

Mrs. Turpin sank back in her chair.

After a moment the girl's eyes closed and she turned her head wearily to the side.

The doctor rose and handed the nurse the empty syringe. He leaned over and put both hands for a moment on the mother's shoulders, which were shaking. She was sitting on the floor, her lips pressed together, holding Mary Grace's hand in her lap. The girl's fingers were gripped like a baby's around her thumb. "Go on to the hospital," he said. "I'll call and make the arrangements."

"Now let's see that neck," he said in a jovial voice to Mrs. Turpin. He began to inspect her neck with his first two fingers. Two little moon-shaped lines like pink fish bones were indented over her windpipe. There was the beginning of an angry red swelling above her eye. His fingers passed over this also.

"Lea' me be," she said thickly and shook him off. "See about Claud. She kicked him."

"I'll see about him in a minute," he said and felt her pulse. He was a thin gray-haired man, given to pleasantries. "Go home and have yourself a vacation the rest of the day," he said and patted her on the shoulder.

Quit your pattin me, Mrs. Turpin growled to herself.

"And put an ice pack over that eye," he said. Then he went and squatted down beside Claud and looked at his leg. After a moment he pulled him up and Claud limped after him into the office.

Until the ambulance came, the only sounds in the room were the tremulous moans of the girl's mother, who continued to sit on the floor. The white-trash woman did not take her eyes off the girl. Mrs. Turpin looked straight ahead at nothing. Presently the ambulance drew up, a long dark shadow, behind the curtain. The attendants came in and set the stretcher down beside the girl and lifted her expertly onto it and carried her out. The nurse helped the mother gather up her things. The shadow of the ambulance moved silently away and the nurse came back in the office.

"That ther girl is going to be a lunatic, ain't she?" the white-trash woman asked the nurse, but the nurse kept on to the back and never answered her.

"Yes, she's going to be a lunatic," the white-trash woman said to the rest of them.

"Po' critter," the old woman murmured. The child's face was still in her lap. His eyes looked idly out over her knees. He had not moved during the disturbance except to draw one leg up under him.

"I thank Gawd," the white-trash woman said fervently, "I ain't a lunatic."

Claud came limping out and the Turpins went home.

As their pick-up truck turned into their own dirt road and made the crest of the hill, Mrs. Turpin gripped the window ledge and looked out suspiciously. The land sloped gracefully down through a field dotted with lavender weeds and at the start of the rise their small yellow frame house, with its little flower beds spread out around it like a fancy apron, sat primly in its accustomed place between two giant hickory trees. She would not have been startled to see a burnt wound between two blackened chimneys.

Neither of them felt like eating so they put on their house clothes and lowered the shade in the bedroom and lay down, Claud with his leg on a pillow and herself with a damp washcloth over her eye. The instant she was flat on her back, the image of a razor-backed hog with warts on its face and horns coming out behind its ears snorted into her head. She moaned, a low quiet moan.

"I am not," she said tearfully, "a wart hog. From hell." But the denial had no force. The girl's eyes and her words, even the tone of her voice, low but clear, directed only to her, brooked no repudiation. She had been singled out for the message, though there was trash in the room to whom it might justly have been applied. The full force of this fact struck her only now. There was a woman there who was neglecting her own child but she had been overlooked. The message had been given to Ruby Turpin, a respectable, hard-working, church-going woman. The tears dried. Her eyes began to burn instead with wrath.

She rose on her elbow and the washcloth fell into her hand. Claud was lying on his back, snoring. She wanted to tell him what the girl had said. At the same time, she did not wish to put the image of herself as a wart hog from hell into his mind.

"Hey, Claud," she muttered and pushed his shoulder.

Claud opened one pale baby blue eye.

She looked into it warily. He did not think about anything. He just went his way.

"Wha, whasit?" he said and closed the eye again.

"Nothing," she said. "Does your leg pain you?"

"Hurts like hell," Claud said.

"It'll quit terreckly," she said and lay back down. In a moment Claud was snoring again. For the rest of the afternoon they lay there. Claud slept. She scowled at the ceiling. Occasionally she raised her fist and made a small stabbing motion over her chest as if she was defending her innocence to invisible guests who were like the comforters of Job, reasonable-seeming but wrong.

About five-thirty Claud stirred. "Got to go after those niggers," he sighed, not moving.

She was looking straight up as if there were unintelligible handwriting on the ceiling. The protuberance over her eye had turned a greenish-blue. "Listen here," she said.

"What?"

"Kiss me."

Claud leaned over and kissed her loudly on the mouth. He pinched her side and their hands interlocked. Her expression of ferocious concentration did not change. Claud got up, groaning and growling, and limped off. She continued to study the ceiling.

She did not get up until she heard the pick-up truck coming back with the Negroes. Then she rose and thrust her feet in her brown oxfords, which she did not bother to lace, and stumped out onto the back porch and got her red plastic bucket. She emptied a tray of ice cubes into it and filled it half full of water and went out into the back yard. Every afternoon after Claud brought the hands in, one of the boys helped him put out hay and the rest waited in the back of the truck until he was ready to take them home. The truck was parked in the shade under one of the hickory trees.

"Hi yawl this evening?" Mrs. Turpin asked grimly, appearing with the bucket and the dipper. There were three women and a boy in the truck.

"Us doin nicely," the oldest woman said. "Hi you doin?" and her gaze stuck immediately on the dark lump on Mrs. Turpin's forehead. "You done fell down, ain't you?" she asked in a solicitous voice. The old woman was dark and almost toothless. She had on an old felt hat of Claud's set back on her head. The other two women were younger and lighter and they both had new bright green sunhats. One of them had hers on her head; the other had taken hers off and the boy was grinning beneath it.

Mrs. Turpin set the bucket down on the floor of the truck. "Yawl hep yourselves," she said. She looked around to make sure Claud had gone. "No, I didn't fall down," she said, folding her arms. "It was something worse than that."

"Ain't nothing bad happen to you!" the old woman said. She said it as if they all knew that Mrs. Turpin was protected in some special way by Divine Providence. "You just had you a little fall."

"We were in town at the doctor's office for where the cow kicked Mr. Turpin," Mrs. Turpin said in a flat tone that indicated they could leave off their foolishness. "And there was this girl there. A big fat girl with her face all broke out. I could look at that girl and tell she was peculiar but I couldn't tell how. And me and her mama was just talking and going along and all of a sudden WHAM! She throws this big book she was reading at me and . . ."

"Naw!" the old woman cried out.

"And then she jumps over the table and commences to choke me."

"Naw!" they all exclaimed, "naw!"

"Hi come she do that?" the old woman asked. "What ail her?" Mrs. Turpin only glared in front of her.

"Somethin ail her," the old woman said.

"They carried her off in an ambulance," Mrs. Turpin continued, "but before she went she was rolling on the floor and they were trying to hold her down to give her a shot and she said something to me." She paused. "You know what she said to me?"

"What she say?" they asked.

"She said," Mrs. Turpin began, and stopped, her face very dark and heavy. The sun was getting whiter and whiter, blanching the sky overhead so that the leaves of the hickory tree were black in the face of it. She could not bring forth the words. "Something real ugly," she muttered.

"She sho shouldn't said nothing ugly to you," the old woman said. "You so sweet. You the sweetest lady I know."

"She pretty too," the one with the hat on said.

"And stout," the other one said. "I never knowed no sweeter white lady."

"That's the truth befo' Jesus," the old woman said. "Amen! You des as sweet and pretty as you can be."

Mrs. Turpin knew exactly how much Negro flattery was worth and it added to her rage. "She said," she began again and finished this time with a fierce rush of breath, "that I was an old wart hog from hell."

There was an astounded silence.

"Where she at?" the youngest woman cried in a piercing voice. "Lemme see her. I'll kill her!"

"I'll kill her with you!" the other one cried.

"She b'long in the sylum," the old woman said emphatically. "You the sweetest white lady I know."

"She pretty too," the other two said. "Stout as she can be and sweet. Jesus satisfied with her!"

"Deed he is," the old woman declared.

Idiots! Mrs. Turpin growled to herself. You could never say anything intelligent to a nigger. You could talk at them but not with them. "Yawl ain't drunk your water," she said shortly. "Leave the bucket in the truck when you're finished with it. I got more to do than just stand around and pass the time of day," and she moved off and into the house.

She stood for a moment in the middle of the kitchen. The dark protuberance over her eye looked like a miniature tornado cloud which might any moment sweep across the horizon of her brow. Her lower lip protruded dangerously. She squared her massive shoulders. Then she marched into the front of the house and out the side door and started down the road to the pig parlor. She had the look of a woman going single-handed, weaponless, into battle.

The sun was a deep yellow now like a harvest moon and was riding westward very fast over the far tree line as if it meant to reach the hogs before she did. The road was rutted and she kicked several good-sized stones out of her path as she strode along. The pig parlor was on a little knoll at the end of a lane that ran off from the side of the barn. It was a square of concrete as large as a small room, with a board fence about four feet high around it. The concrete floor sloped slightly so that the hog wash could drain off into a trench where it was carried to the field for fertilizer. Claud was standing on the outside, on the edge of the concrete, hanging onto the top board, hosing down the floor inside. The hose was connected to the faucet of a water trough nearby.

Mrs. Turpin climbed up beside him and glowered down at the hogs inside. There were seven long-snouted bristly shoats in it—tan with liver-colored spots—and an old sow a few weeks off from farrowing. She was lying on her side grunting. The shoats were running about shaking themselves like idiot children, their little slit pig eyes searching the floor for anything left. She had read that pigs were the most intelligent animal. She doubted it. They were supposed to be smarter than dogs. There had even been a pig astronaut. He had performed his assignment perfectly but died of a heart attack afterwards because they left him in his electric suit, sitting upright throughout his examination when naturally a hog should be on all fours.

A-gruntin and a-rootin and a-groanin.

"Gimme that hose," she said, yanking it away from Claud. "Go on and carry them niggers home and then get off that leg."

"You look like you might have swallowed a mad dog," Claud observed, but he got down and limped off. He paid no attention to her humors.

Until he was out of earshot, Mrs. Turpin stood on the side of the pen, holding the hose and pointing the stream of water at the hind quarters of any shoat that looked as if it might try to lie down. When he had had time to get over the hill, she turned her head slightly and her wrathful eyes scanned the path. He was nowhere in sight. She turned back again and seemed to gather herself up. Her shoulders rose and she drew in her breath.

"What do you send me a message like that for?" she said in a low fierce voice, barely above a whisper but with the force of a shout in its concentrated fury. "How am I a hog and me both? How am I saved and from hell too?" Her free fist was knotted and with the other she gripped the hose, blindly pointing the stream of water in and out of the eye of the old sow whose outraged squeal she did not hear.

The pig parlor commanded a view of the back pasture where their twenty beef cows were gathered around the hay-bales Claud and the boy had put out. The freshly cut pasture sloped down to the highway. Across it was their cotton field and beyond that a dark green dusty wood which they owned as well. The sun was behind the wood, very red, looking over the paling of trees like a farmer inspecting his own hogs.

"Why me?" she rumbled. "It's no trash around here, black or white, that I haven't given to. And break my back to the bone every day working. And do for the church."

She appeared to be the right size woman to command the arena before her. "How am I a hog?" she demanded. "Exactly how am I like them?" and she jabbed the stream of water at the shoats. "There was plenty of trash there. It didn't have to be me.

"If you like trash better, go get yourself some trash then," she railed. "You could have made me trash. Or a nigger. If trash is what you wanted why didn't you make me trash?" She shook her fist with the hose in it and a watery snake appeared momentarily in the air. "I could quit working and take it easy and be filthy," she growled. "Lounge about the sidewalks all day drinking root beer. Dip snuff and spit in every puddle and have it all over my face. I could be nasty.

"Or you could have made me a nigger. It's too late for me to be a nigger," she said with deep sarcasm, "but I could act like one. Lay down in the middle of the road and stop traffic. Roll on the ground."

In the deepening light everything was taking on a mysterious hue. The pasture was growing a peculiar glassy green and the streak of highway had turned lavender. She braced herself for a final assault and this time her voice rolled out over the pasture. "Go on," she yelled, "call me a hog! Call me a hog again. From hell. Call me a wart hog from hell. Put that bottom rail on top. There'll still be a top and bottom!"

A garbled echo returned to her.

A final surge of fury shook her and she roared, "Who do you think you are?"

The color of everything, field and crimson sky, burned for a moment with a transparent intensity. The question carried over the pasture and across the highway and the cotton field and returned to her clearly like an answer from beyond the wood.

She opened her mouth but no sound came out of it.

A tiny truck, Claud's, appeared on the highway, heading rapidly out of sight. Its gears scraped thinly. It looked like a child's toy. At any moment a bigger truck might smash into it and scatter Claud's and the niggers' brains all over the road.

Mrs. Turpin stood there, her gaze fixed on the highway, all her muscles rigid, until in five or six minutes the truck reappeared, returning. She waited until it had had time to turn into their own road. Then like a monumental statue coming to life, she bent her head slowly and gazed, as if through the very heart of mystery, down into the pig parlor at the hogs. They had settled all in one corner around the old sow who was grunting softly. A red glow suffused them. They appeared to pant with a secret life.

Until the sun slipped finally behind the tree line, Mrs. Turpin remained there with her gaze bent to them as if she were absorbing some abysmal life-giving knowledge. At last she lifted her head. There was only a purple streak in the sky, cutting through a field of crimson and leading, like an extension of the highway, into the descending dusk. She raised her hands from the side of the pen in a gesture hieratic and profound. A visionary light settled in her eyes. She saw the streak as a vast swinging bridge extending upward from the earth through a field of living fire. Upon it a vast horde of souls were rumbling toward heaven. There were whole companies of white-trash, clean for the first time in their lives, and bands of black niggers in white robes, and battalions of freaks and lunatics shouting and clapping and leaping like frogs. And bringing up the end of the procession was a tribe of people whom she recognized at once as those who, like herself and Claud, had always had a little of everything and the God-given wit to use it right. She leaned forward to observe them closer. They were marching behind the others with great dignity, accountable as they had always been for good order and common sense and respectable behavior. They alone were on key. Yet she could see by their shocked and altered faces that even their virtues were being burned away. She lowered her hands and gripped the rail of the hog pen, her eyes small but fixed unblinkingly on what lay ahead. In a moment the vision faded but she remained where she was, immobile.

At length she got down and turned off the faucet and made her slow way on the darkening path to the house. In the woods around her the invisible cricket choruses had struck up, but what she heard were the voices of the souls climbing upward into the starry field and shouting hallelujah.

A Poem About Angels

❧ JACQUELINE OSCHEROW

You want to write a poem about angels.
Not because they are winged and white and haloed
And in many paintings very beautiful
But because you have seen many things and remembered
Only angels. You are certain, for example,
That you walked on famous streets,
Under towers, over rivers, around the parapets
Of ancient walls, medieval walls.

Once, you watched beeches turn to cypress
From a moving train, and every time you looked,
Another season. Surely there were mountains
By the side of the road. You wrote it down.

Only the angels are intact, marble
Or otherwise, recorded, you imagine, before breakfast,
Maybe before dawn, by some lucky visionary
With a paintbrush. You believed especially
The story of the man who fell asleep and woke
To find his Mary finished by the angels.
You would like to know those thorough angels
With names like Gabriel, the cherubim, the seraphim.

All you know is how impossible it is
Without them. The stones conspire against you

With the heavy clouds, and everything through glass
Or, worse, that cracking memory, flashing tents
And camels in between the high pink towns
Of, was it Tuscany, as if the slides you never took
Got all mixed up. Only occasional the empty screen
For you to fill with all your angels.

In the dim church, a darker patch of wall,
The handiwork of angels. A face
More gentle than the finished circle
Of a moon altering your courtyard,
Unhinging buildings from their heavy stones.

The angels could help you with anything.
They could show you how to use a word like *dream*
Or *I* in the middle of a poem, pressing you
With secrets like their oldest friends,
Prophets, patriarchs, and kings.

Still, they're busy with gardening
And God to deal with who is old
And must be disappointed. I suppose
The scenery gets dull, if you're
An angel. All that cloud and pearl.
There aren't chariots of fire
Every day, you know, and it's a long time
Between appearances in dreams.

One night, they are gathered on a cloud.
A moon, completed, rises, catches them off guard
And before they think that is another month
And I have done nothing, one cries, "Gabriel,
Look, Gabriel." And Gabriel, transformed,
Puts down his harp, which he has been playing
Only mechanically for the last two weeks,
And hums a long-dreamed psalm.

Grateful acknowledgment is made to the following for permission to reprint previously published material:

The American-Scandinavian Foundation: "The Wish" by Einar Kvaran. Reprinted by permission of The American-Scandinavian Foundation.

Ballantine Books: Excerpt from *A Book of Angels* by Sophy Burnham. Copyright © 1990 by Sophy Burnham. Reprinted by permission of Ballantine Books, a division of Random House, Inc.

Bantam Books: Excerpt from *The Divine Comedy of Dante Alighieri: Purgatorio* by Allen Mandelbaum. Translation copyright © 1982 by Allen Mandelbaum. Reprinted by permission of Bantam Books, a division of Bantam Doubleday Dell Publishing Group, Inc.

Curtis Brown Ltd.: Five poems from *Two-Headed Woman* by Lucille Clifton. Copyright © 1980 by University of Massachusetts Press. Reprinted by permission of Curtis Brown Ltd.

Farrar, Straus & Giroux, Inc.: "Seascape" and "Invitation to Miss Marianne Moore" from *The Complete Poems 1927–1979* by Elizabeth Bishop. Copyright © 1979, 1983 by Alice Helen Methfessel. "Angel Levine" from *The Magic Barrel* by Bernard Malamud. Copyright © 1955, 1958, and copyright renewed © 1986 by Bernard Malamud. Excerpt from a letter to "A," 17 January 1956 from *The Habit of Being* by Flannery O'Connor, edited by Sally Fitzgerald. Copyright © 1979 by Regina O'Connor. Reprinted by permission of Farrar, Straus & Giroux, Inc.

Harcourt Brace & Company: "A Still Moment" from *The Wide Net and Other Stories* by Eudora Welty. Copyright 1942 and renewed 1970 by Eudora Welty. "Monday or Tuesday" from *A Haunted House and Other Short Stories* by Virginia Woolf. Copyright 1944 and renewed 1972 by Harcourt Brace & Company. "Professions for Women" from *The Death of the Moth and Other Essays* by Virginia Woolf. Copyright © 1942 by Harcourt Brace & Company and renewed 1970 by Marjorie T. Parsons, Executrix. "Love Calls Us to the Things of This World" from *Things of This World* by Richard Wilbur. Copyright © 1956 and renewed 1984 by Richard Wilbur. "Revelation" from *The Complete Stories* by Flannery O'Connor. Copyright © 1964, 1965, 1971 by the Estate of Mary Flannery O'Connor. Reprinted by permission of Harcourt Brace & Company.

HarperCollins Publishers Inc.: "The Visit" from *Baptism of Desire* by Louise Erdrich. Copyright © 1990 by Louise Erdrich. "Black Rock in Rainy Weather" from *The Collected Poems of Sylvia Plath* edited by Ted Hughes. Copyright © 1960, 1965, 1971, and 1981 by the Estate of Sylvia Plath. "A Very Old Man with Enormous Wings" from *The Collected Stories of Gabriel García Márquez*. Copyright © 1984 by Gabriel García Márquez. Reprinted by permission of HarperCollins Publishers Inc.

Houghton Mifflin Company: "Angel of Blizzards and Blackouts" from *The Book of Folly* by Anne Sexton. Copyright © 1972 by Anne Sexton. Reprinted by permission of Houghton Mifflin Co. All rights reserved.

Alfred A. Knopf, Inc.: "Angel" and "A Dedication" from *Selected Poems 1946–1985* by James Merrill. Copyright © 1992 by James Merrill. Excerpt from *Stories in an Almost Classical Mode* by Harold Brodkey. Copyright © 1988 by Harold Brodkey. "Evening Without Angels" and "An-

ABOUT THE AUTHOR

HARRIET SCOTT CHESSMAN taught English and American literature at Yale University for eleven years. She has written on twentieth-century literature and painting. Most recently, she published a book on the writing of Gertrude Stein, *The Public Is Invited to Dance*. She now writes children's books and is at work on her first novel. She lives in Madison, Connecticut.